The Spirited Baker
Intoxicating Desserts
& Potent Potables

Marie Porter

Photography by
Michael Porter

Celebration Generation

www.celebrationgeneration.com

The Spirited Baker

Second Edition, June 2013

I.S.B.N. 978-0-9846040-3-6

Published and Distributed by

Celebration Generation
P.O. Box 22315
Robbinsdale, MN USA
55422

www.celebrationgeneration.com

Cover Photos, Clockwise from Top left:

Raspberry-Peach Bread Pudding, page 94
Creme de Menthe Nanaimo Bars , page 150
Sangria Poached Pears, page 178
Jalapeno Beer Baklava, page 123
Kiwi Liqueur - Infusions and Liqueurs, page 12

Back Cover Photo:

Peachy Southern Comfort Cheesecake, page 30

Acknowledgments

Who ever knew that writing a cook book could be so mentally and physically taxing? I would like to acknowledge and extend my heartfelt gratitude to the following persons who have made the completion of this book possible. They were there for me through constant battles with ADD and my penchant for procrastination, and I appreciate it all more than I can actually describe here.

Specifically...

My husband and photographer, Porter. The most sweet, stubborn, romantic, bull-headed, awesome, frustrating, cute, smart, talented, nerdy, and fun man I've ever known. I love you :)

My grandmother, for raising me right. You are the calm - and sane! - in the eye of our family's storms, and your kindness, generosity, and patience were not lost on me! Thank you for everything.

Janet, Beth Anne, Cynthia, Robin, Michael, and everyone else on the 'WeeM teem for the past few years. You guys are fabulousness incarnate, and it's been great working with you. Rock stars, all of you.

I'm definitely more of a sprinter than a marathoner, so my focus and drive to finish this book took a lot of extra support. I can't tell you how many energy drinks and shots I've consumed in the past 2 years! In addition to liquid focus, I really need to thank the Morning Show, Hammer, DJ Danny D, and Tony Monaco at z103.5 for providing a such great stream of tunes. Ah, I love the internet... I've really counted on you guys for my steady diet of eurodance. Wednesdays have been my most productive days for a reason!

Finally - Let's be serious here, there is no way that this book would have been seen through to fruition without Ritalin. Attention Deficit Disorder has seriously impacted the course my life has taken, and it's been a constant battle for me. I'd like to thank Novartis for their part in my having any ability to focus at all. Without the help of Ritalin, there is no way that this book would have been completed, no matter how much emotional support I've received elsewhere.

Table of Contents

Page

Foreword 7

Let's Get it Started 9

Creamy 40

Cakey 57

Fancy 105

Munchy 142

Fruity 169

Conversions 189

Resources 190

Index 191

Foreword

The way I am figuring it, there are two main reactions that this book will receive.

1. "Wow, what a cool idea!" This is the reaction I've had tons of exposure to, whether online, at the farmer's market, or people I talk to.

2. "What kind of a lush writes a book like THAT?" I have not received this reaction yet (to my face, anyway!), but I'm sure it's out there.

Yup, I could see it being very easy to write this book off as some serious lushiness... but let me explain. This, my first cookbook, has been a long time coming. It's the now-obvious perfect extension of many years of circumstance and aptitude.

Like many bakers, I started early. In the beginning, there was the toy oven. The mixes were horrendous, and the end product.. not entirely edible. I graduated to the real oven fairly early on. Oh how I loved messing around, coming up with new ideas. I loved to create.

Around the same time, I developed an interesting collecting hobby. While many kids my age collected stickers, shells, trading cards, or whatever.. I'd collect mini bottles of liqueurs. Empty, of course - I just liked the aromas. I know I had a pretty varied collection, but I remember clearly how much I loved the smell of Peach Schnapps and Creme De Menthe in particular. How classy, right?

I grew up, honed my talents in baking and design, and eventually forgot about my collection. Had my first drinking experience - and first hangover - fairly early, and decided that I didn't get the attraction of drinking to get drunk. Camping out by a toilet and wishing for death to come fast is a long ways away from that simple joy of smelling an empty bottle!

Still don't get it.

While I never did develop a taste for beer, or for hard spirits straight up, I did develop a taste for girlie cocktails. I loved the complex flavor profiles that could be achieved through mixology, and it worked well with my aptitude for experimentation. My career path evolved from wedding gown design, to floral design, to graphic design... and finally landing on custom cake design. Somewhere along the line, I took an extensive series of courses on bartending.

My first attempt at combining bartending and baking yielded an amazing pina colada Bundt cake - and you'll find that recipe in this book! That was back when I was baking just for fun. Eventually I opened my cake business, and a lot of experimentation went into developing
my flavor menu. I didn't want to be one of those "White, chocolate, marble, or spice" businesses. It was fun coming up with an exciting and inspiring menu.. and it was fun to see the look of wonder on my brides' faces. Kids in a candy store, choosing their perfect wedding cake.

The thing about baking with liqueurs is that it really opens up the flavor possibilities.

Introducing flavors to your baking, in the form of liquid, is very convenient. There are very few things you can do with solid flavoring agents, that wouldn't alter that texture or general appearance of the final product. Extracts can be a great option, but selection at the average grocery store is extremely limiting. Rum, coconut, cherry, banana, mint, almond, and lemon.. Usually.

However, if you go to any liquor store- and look at their selection of liqueurs as flavoring agents - you have a whole new world of options. You have many more "basic" flavors.. black walnut, peach, pomegranate, orange, raspberry and more.. As well as a new variety of more complex flavors. Irish cream, Southern Comfort, strawberry cream tequila. The possibilities are endless!

Combining these new flavoring agents with more traditional baking ingredients can yield spectacular results. Southern comfort, peaches, and almonds create an amazing cheesecake. Rum, mangoes, and fresh mint combine to make a wild "Mango mojito upside down cake"... and so much more.

This book is a great introduction to using the various available liqueurs and spirits as flavoring agents In many cases, you can adjust the amount of alcohol vs other liquid to create stronger or more subtle effects. I hope you - and your friends - enjoy this book and the goodies you'll make.

Please drink - and munch! - responsibly!

-Marie

Let's Get it Started

This book is a complete guide to making a variety of amazing desserts, using ingredients that are readily available at your local grocery and liquor stores.

This chapter, however, is all about creating your own ingredients. Yes, you can buy ready-made simple syrup, sweet and sour mix, grenadine, and any number of liqueurs. You can buy a variety of basic flavor extracts at any grocery store.. but really, it's so much more fun, economical - and tasty - to make your own!

When it comes to infusing spirits, creating liqueurs, and crafting your own extracts, you'll want to start well in advance of your baking project. The day before you want to bake a cake is not the time to decide that you want to use a custom liqueur! Many need to infuse for several weeks, so be sure to plan ahead.

When it comes to the non-alcohol ingredients, such as grenadine, simple syrup, and sweet & sour mix: It's always good to keep some on hand, in your fridge. Aside from being great ingredients to bake these recipes with, they're handy for cocktail making. Just be forewarned: Once you've tried fresh ingredients, you'll have a very hard time settling for their commercially available counterparts in the future!

Liqueur Making

When looking to the liquor store as a source of flavors for your baking, you'll be blown away by all of the possibilities. Whether you grab a bottle of Chambord or a coconut rum, a good liquor store can provide a great variety of ingredients to play with.

What happens when you get bored ... or if you're stuck with a liquor store that carries an inadequate variety of liqueurs? You make your own!

Infusing spirits and/or making your own liqueurs at home really opens up a world of possibilities. It's easy, cheap, and rewarding. Let your imagination run wild, and experiment with different spirits and flavorings. Whether you're aiming for an elegant, refined taste (Rose petals and plums!), "Knock your socks off" (Jalapeno tequila!), or just weird (Skittles flavored vodka?)... the sky really is the limit. Pretty much any fruit, nut, herb, or spice can be infused into any spirit - it's largely just a matter of personal preference.

Various Infused Spirits

Before you start, a few tips:

- Start by choosing the flavor you'd like. A fruit? Nut? Herb? Combination of the above? If using more than one flavor, what kind of proportions do you want? The next consideration is the spirit that you will be infusing. Think about the flavor of the spirit, the flavor you'll be infusing... and also about the final intended use of your infused spirit.

- If you're looking to really showcase the flavor of the fruit/nut/ etc, you'll want to choose a spirit that is fairly light, and possibly neutral. Vodka works beautifully for almost any flavor. Light rum can be a great base for many fruit or nut flavors in particular, and gin can provide a
nice canvas for berries and botanical ingredients.

- Brandy and whisky can also be used, but because they have big flavor on their own, you'll want to plan around that. Either plan for a brandy or whiskey with just a hint of flavor infused, or pick big, robust flavors to infuse.

- Wines and sakes can also be infused with flavor. Try a fruity infusion with honey wine, fresh ginger in sake.. It's all good.

- For any of the recipes, feel free to tinker. Substitute a different spirit, add more of a flavoring agent, add an extra ingredient, whatever.

- If your infusion lacks flavor even after steeping for a couple of weeks, just add more of your flavoring agents, and continue infusing until it's just right!

- If your infusion has too strong of a flavor after steeping, just add a little more spirit, to taste. Allowing infusion to age is important in this case!

- If planning to dilute the spirit later, either as a liqueur or a cream liqueur, aim for a stronger taste in the initial infusion.

- Be sure to wash all fruits, vegetables, and herbs before infusing.

- The more surface area, the easier the flavor will extract. For this reason, you'll want to chop large pieces into smaller chunks.

- Use clean mason jars with tight fitting lids.

- I like to strain the infused spirit first with a fine mesh strainer, then a second time through a coffee filter.

- Once your infusion is strained and bottled, you should let it age for about a week in the fridge before drinking it. IF you have that kind of patience! Aging results in a smoother, more mellow flavor.

Infused Spirit Recipes & Inspiration

For each recipe:

- Place all ingredients into jar(s), cap tightly.
- Shake filled jars a few times every day during the infusion process.
- Taste for doneness.
- Once desired flavor strength is achieved, strain spirit and bottle into clean jars / bottles, or use to make liqueur or cream liqueur

Fruit Infused Spirits

Vodka, rum, or whatever	3 cups	750 ml
Fresh fruit	1 - 1 ½ cups	250 - 375 ml

Prepare fruit:

Wash, leave peels on, chop: Apples, blood oranges, grapefruit, lemons, limes, nectarines, oranges, peaches, pears

Wash, chop, slice, and/or lightly mash: Blackberries, blueberries, cranberries, raspberries, strawberries

Wash, remove pit/core, chop fruit: Apricots, cherries, mango, nectarines, peaches, pineapple, plums

Remove shell, chop fruit: Coconut

Peel, seed, chop fruit: Cantaloupe, honeydew, watermelon

Peel, chop fruit: Kiwi

Infusion time will vary by fruit. As a general guideline:

1 week:	Blood oranges, grapefruit, lemons, limes, oranges
2 weeks:	Blackberries, blueberries, cherries, cranberries, kiwi, mangoes, nectarines, peaches, plums, raspberries, strawberries
3 weeks:	Apricots, apples, cantaloupe, honeydew, pears, watermelon
4+ weeks:	Coconut, pineapple

Kiwi Infused Vodka

Peanut Infused Rum

Amber or dark rum	3 cups	750 ml
Unsalted, roasted peanuts	2 cups	500 ml

Allow to infuse for approximately 2 weeks.

Coffee Infused Vodka

Good quality vodka	3 cups	750 ml
Dark roast coffee beans, smashed.	½ cup	125 ml

Allow to infuse for approximately 5 days.

Spice Infused Vodka

Good quality vodka	3 cups	750 ml
Whole dry spices*	1/4 cup	50 ml

*Anise seed, star anise, cinnamon sticks, cardamom, nutmeg, etc

Allow to infuse for approximately 2-5 days, tasting daily.

Herb Infused Vodka

Good quality vodka	3 cups	750 ml
Fresh herbs*	½ cup	125 ml

*Rosemary, mint, basil, dill, whatever

Allow to infuse for approximately 3-5 days, tasting daily.

Skittles Infused Vodka

Good quality vodka	3 cups	750 ml
ONE FLAVOR of skittles	½ cup	125 ml

Allow to infuse for approximately 1-2 days.

Jalapeno Infused Tequila

Good quality tequila	3 cups	750 ml
Jalapeno peppers, chopped	4	4

Allow to infuse for approximately 3 days.

Cucumber Infused Vodka

Good quality vodka	3 cups	750 ml
Large cucumbers, chopped	1-2	1-2

Allow to infuse for approximately 1-2 weeks.

Rose Infused Vodka

Good quality vodka	3 cups	750 ml
Organic rose petals, chopped	1-2 cups	250-500 ml

Allow to infuse for approximately 1-2 weeks.

NB: This is also great with a bit of lemon or orange peel and/or a couple tsp dried lavender added in!

Tea Infused Vodka

Good quality vodka	3 cups	750 ml
Whole tea (Or 4-5 tea bags)	3 tbsp	45 ml

Allow to infuse for approximately 2 days

Chai Infused Vodka

Good quality vodka	3 cups	750 ml
Whole masala chai	5 Tbsp	75 ml

Allow to infuse for 1-2 days

Green Tea Infused Vodka

| Good quality vodka | 3 cups | 750 ml |
| Green tea leaves | 3 Tbsp | 45 ml |

Allow to infuse for 1-2 days

Vanilla Infused Vodka

| Good quality vodka | 3 cups | 750 ml |
| Vanilla beans | 2-3 | 2-3 |

Slice beans in half lengthwise. Allow to infuse approximately 5 days.

Ginger Infused Vodka

| Good quality vodka | 3 cups | 750 ml |
| Peeled, chopped ginger | 1/4 -1/2 cup | 50-125 ml |

Allow to infuse approximately 2-3 weeks

Fig Infused Brandy

| Good quality brandy | 3 cups | 750 ml |
| Chopped figs (fresh or dried) | 1 cup | 250 ml |

Allow to infuse approximately 1 month.

Think you've got the hang of it? Try experimenting! Here are a few ideas to play with:

Lemon & fresh ginger   *   Lemon & rosemary   *   Plum & rose petal

Tea & lemon   * Cranberries & orange   *   Peach & raspberry

Pineapple & vanilla   *   Lime & ginger   *   Kiwi & pineapple

Pineapple & coconut

Liqueurs

Infused spirits are great for making cocktails, or using in the recipes throughout the rest of this book..Sometimes, though, you just want a special, sweet "sippy" drink. That, my friends, is when liqueur making comes in. This is a very easy process, which also opens up more opportunity for flavor. More on that later.

Basic Liqueur Recipe

1 - 2 parts infused spirit
1 part simple syrup

Combine ingredients, taste. Adjust ingredients for desired sweetness, bottle. Allow to age for about 1 month in the fridge before drinking - IF you have that kind of patience.

See? Very simple. Of course, you don't need to stop there. Shortly, I'll be equipping you with not one, but several syrup recipes. Mix and match your infused spirits with the various syrups for a myriad of potential combinations. Sweet and Sour mix, Lime Cordial, and Grenadine can all be used in place of part of the simple syrup measure as well!

Flavor Ideas:

Sweet Tea - Tea infused vodka with either simple or honey syrup. Substitute a bit of lemon based sweet and sour for some of the simple syrup for a lemon iced tea!

Maple Vanilla Liqueur - Vanilla infused vodka with maple simple syrup. Use ½ maple simple syrup, ½ regular simple syrup if you'd like a more subtle maple flavor.

Peanut Liqueur - Peanut infused rum with either simple or brown sugar simple syrup.

Cucumber Melon Liqueur - Mix 1 part each Cantaloupe and Cucumber infused vodka, with 1 part simple syrup.

Ginger Green Tea Liqueur - Start with a base of green tea infused vodka. Add ginger infused vodka to taste. Mix in simple syrup to taste.

Blueberry Liqueur, With Added Blueberries for Presentation

Simple Syrups

Simple syrup is used in many cocktails, as well as an ingredient in baking. Simple syrup may be infused to create flavored syrups - often used as garnish, or to add additional flavor or moisture to baked goods.

Basic Simple Syrup
1 part water
1 part sugar*

Heavy Simple Syrup
1 part water
2 parts sugar*

Combine water and sugar in a saucepan. Heat to boiling, stirring until sugar is dissolved. Remove from heat and cool before using. Store unused syrup in fridge.

* Brown sugar may be substituted. This will add a richer, "molasses" taste to anything the syrup is used on/in. Keep in mind, though: the darker color of brown sugar simple syrup will alter the color of any cocktails it is used in.

Honey or Maple Simple Syrup

These variations can be used in place of simple syrup to add a bit of flavor in almost any recipe.

Honey Simple Syrup
1 part water
1 part honey

Maple Simple Syrup
1 part water
1 part pure maple syrup

Combine water and honey or maple syrup in a saucepan. Heat to a simmer, stirring until syrup is dissolved. Remove from heat and cool before using. Store unused syrup in fridge.

Cream Liqueur Recipe

1 cup heavy cream	1 cup	250 ml
Sweetened condensed milk	14 oz	400 g
Infused spirit	1 ½ cups	375 ml
Chocolate, chopped (optional)		

Combine heavy cream and sweetened condensed milk in a saucepan. Heat to a simmer, stirring constantly. If adding chocolate (as much or as little as you want), mix in at this point, stirring until melted and completely incorporated into cream. Remove from heat, allow to cool.

In a blender, mixer, or food processor, blend cooled milk mixture with infused spirit. Beat/blend on high for about 2 minutes to emulsify the mixture. Bottle, store in fridge. Use within 1 month, giving bottle a good shake if any separation has occurred. Much like everything else in this book, you can definitely play with this recipe. Any of the simple syrups can be substituted for ½ of the heavy cream, for instance. Use chocolate, or don't. Use any type of chocolate. Whatever floats your boat!

Flavor ideas:

- Raspberry infused vodka with white chocolate
- Coffee infused liqueur with dark chocolate
- Mango infused rum with a bit of brown sugar simple syrup
- Green tea infused vodka, no chocolate.
- Blood orange infused vodka with a bit of dark or milk chocolate

Grenadine

Yes, grenadine is readily available in grocery and liquor stores. It's definitely a viable alternative if you don't have the time or inclination to make your own. Once you've had the homemade version, though - you'll never buy grenadine again! In addition to having a more pure, clean pomegranate taste, the homemade version also lacks the high fructose corn syrup and other additives found in commercially available grenadine. Incidently, while grenadine is supposed to be a pomegranate syrup, the vast majority of retail varieties contain no actual pomegranate. Such a shame!

Pomegranate juice*	2 cups	500 ml
Sugar	1 cup	250 ml

Heat to juice to boiling, turn heat down and simmer until reduced to about half the original volume. Add sugar, stirring until dissolved. Remove from heat and cool before using. Store unused syrup in fridge.

* While pomegranate is most traditional, feel free to experiment with different flavors! This recipe also yields beautiful results from cherry, blueberry, and raspberry juices.

Milk and White Chocolate Cream Liqueurs

Lime Cordial

Lime cordial is a sweetened lime juice syrup, most commonly available as "Rose's Lime". Everything I said about grenadine? Applies here too!

Water	1 ½ cups	375 ml
Sugar	1 cup	250 ml
Citric acid	3/4 tsp	3 ml
Tartaric acid	1/4 tsp	1 ml
Lime juice *	1 cup	250 ml
Peel from 3 limes		

Combine water, sugar, citric acid and tartaric acid in a saucepan. Heat to boiling, stirring until sugar is dissolved. Add lime juice and peels, bring to a boil. Turn heat down, simmer mixture for 5 minutes. Remove from heat and cool. Once syrup is cooled, strain syrup to remove lime rind. Store unused syrup in fridge.

* Freshly squeezed juice is always best!

Sweet and Sour

Sweet and Sour is also referred to as "bar mix", "bar lime", and "sour mix". Much like grenadine, homemade sweet and sour is much better than store bought, both in taste and nutritionally speaking.

Water	3 cups	750 ml
Sugar	3 cups	750 ml
Lemon juice *	2 cups	500 ml
Lime juice *	2 cups	500 ml

Combine water and sugar in a saucepan. Heat to boiling, stirring until sugar is dissolved. Remove from heat and cool. Once syrup is cooled, add lemon and lime juices, stir well. Store unused syrup in fridge for no more than 2 weeks.

* Freshly squeezed juice is always best! Also, you can play with amounts and type of juices used. Try 3 cups (750 ml) lime and 1 cup (250 ml) lemon juice for a great margarita mix. Substitute orange juice for some of the lemon and/or lime juice for an interesting citrus mix.

Lime Cordial

Flavor Extracts

Making flavor extracts at home can be rewarding on several levels. It can be more economical, provide a better tasting product, provide *more* of a product (convenience!), and also allow for a greater variety.

Pure flavor extracts are usually fairly simple: just an alcohol base, used to extract flavors from a fruit, nut, spice, or whatever. Lemon extract can be made with lemon peels and vodka. Vanilla extract from vanilla beans, and so forth.

There are a few differences between infusing for baking extracts, and infusing for spirits and liqueurs. The reason for this is the difference in strength of flavor. In general, flavor extracts feature a far more concentrated taste than spirits and liqueurs. While Limoncello is pleasant to sip on, you'd never want to use lemon extract in the same way.

We've already covered infusing alcohol for flavored spirits and liqueurs, but here, we'll address homemade extracts! In addition to being great to use in your own kitchen, any or all of these make excellent gifts.

Vanilla Extract

Good quality vodka	3 cups	750 ml
Vanilla beans	8	8

Cut vanilla beans in half, lengthwise. Place in a sterilized glass jar or bottle, cover with vodka. Store in a cool dark place for 2 - 4 months, giving the jar an occasional shake. Strain out the vanilla beans and bottle the extract.

Citrus Extract

Good quality vodka	3 cups	750 ml
Citrus peel	1 - 1 ½ cups	250-375 ml

Wash fruit - lemons, limes, oranges, grapefruit - well before peeling. Using a vegetable peeler, remove the colored rind only - using the white pith can result in an unpleasant taste. Chop peels into small pieces.

Place fruit peels in a sterilized glass or bottle, cover with vodka. Store in a cool dark place for about 5 days, giving the jar an occasional shake. Taste - if extract has reached desired strength, strain out the peels and bottle the extract. If not, allow to steep a few more days and taste again.

Vanilla Extract

Spice Extract

Good quality vodka	3 cups	750 ml
Whole dry spices	½ cup	125 ml

Place spice in a sterilized glass or bottle, cover with vodka. Store in a cool dark place for about 2 months, giving the jar an occasional shake. Taste frequently- when extract has reached desired strength, use a coffee filter (or two!) to strain out the spice, Bottle the extract.

Herbal Extract

Good quality vodka	3 cups	750 ml
Fresh herbs	½ - 1 cup	125-250 ml

Place cleaned herbs in a sterilized glass or bottle, cover with vodka.
Store in a cool dark place for about 1 month, giving the jar an occasional shake. Taste frequently- when extract has reached desired strength, use a coffee filter (or two!) to strain out the herbs. Bottle the extract.

Creamy

Cheesecakes

There are two main components to a cheesecake - the crust, and the "cake" itself. By varying the flavors involved in either or both of these elements, you're afforded an endless amount of dessert possibilities!

Basic Cheesecake Crust

Crumbs *	1 ½ cup	375 ml
Sugar	1/4 cup	50 ml
Butter, melted	5 Tbsp	75 ml

Combine all ingredients until completely incorporated & moistened. Evenly distribute across the bottom of a 9"spring form pan. Press ingredients firmly, extending crust partway up the sides of the pan. Chill for at least 1 hour.

* Crumbs:

- Use graham cracker crumbs for a basic, traditional cheesecake crust.

- Try gingersnap cookies for a more flavorful crust, and to accent spicier cheesecakes (like pumpkin or chai!)

- Oreos, Nilla wafers, or any other type of dry cookie can be used to customize crust flavor

- Substitute finely chopped nuts for all or part of the crumbs: a great tasting, gluten free alternative!

Basic Boozy Cheesecake Batter

Cream cheese, room temperature	2 lbs	1000 g
Sugar	1 ½ cup	375 ml
Sour cream	1 cup	250 ml
Heavy cream	½ cup	125 ml
Cream liqueur of choice*	½ cup	125 ml
Eggs	6	6
Juice of one lemon		

Preheat oven to 425°F (220°C)

In stand mixer, beat together cream cheese and sugar until smooth. Add sour cream, heavy cream, liqueur, eggs, and lemon juice. Beat on low / medium-low until smooth. Gently pour batter into prepared crust. Chill for 10 minutes.

Bake for 15 minutes. After 15 minutes, turn the oven down to 325°F (160° C) and bake for 50 minutes. Once baking time is complete, turn off the oven and allow cake to cool - WITHOUT opening the door! - for 2 hours. Chill cake thoroughly before serving.

* Cream liqueur can be any cream based liqueur of your choice - Bailey's, Godiva, Baja Luna, Tequila Rose, etc. I recommend using the ½ cup liqueur to ½ cup heavy cream proportions, but you can tinker with the amounts to make your flavor more subtle or more robust. Just be sure to keep the total liqueur/cream volume at 1 cup.

If you'd like to use a non-cream based liqueur, use 1/4 cup liqueur with ½ cup heavy cream - the total volume will be 3/4 cup.

Chocolate Chambord Cheesecake

Crust:

Chocolate cookie crumbs	1 ½ cup	375 ml
Sugar	1/4 cup	50 ml
Butter, melted	5 Tbsp	75 ml

Combine all ingredients until completely incorporated & moistened. Evenly distribute across the bottom of a 9" spring form pan. Press ingredients firmly, extending crust partway up the sides of the pan. Chill for at least 1 hour.

Filling:

Bittersweet or semi sweet chocolate	8 oz	225 g
Cream cheese, room temperature	2 lbs	1000 g
Sugar	1 ½ cups	375 ml
Sour cream	1 cup	250 ml
Heavy cream	½ cup	125 ml
Chambord*	1/4 cup	50 ml
Eggs	6	6
juice of one lemon		

Topping:

1 cup raspberries	1 cup	250 ml
½ cup sugar	½ cup	125 ml
1/4 cup Chambord	1/4 cup	50 ml

Preheat oven to 425° (220°C).

Chop chocolate. In a clean, dry glass bowl, melt chocolate in microwave. Be careful not to burn it - I recommend starting with 45 seconds, then 30 second increments, removing bowl before all chocolate is melted. Stir until all chocolate is melted and smooth - set aside to cool slightly.

In stand mixer, beat together cream cheese and sugar until smooth. Add sour cream, heavy cream, Chambord, eggs, and lemon juice. Beat on low / medium-low until smooth. Add cooled melted chocolate, continue beating on low until fully incorporated. Gently pour batter into prepared crust. Chill for 10 minutes.

Bake for 15 minutes. After 15 minutes, turn the oven down to 325°F (160°C) and bake for 50 minutes. Once baking time is complete, turn off the oven and allow cake to cool - WITHOUT opening the door! - for 2 hours. Meanwhile, combine topping ingredients in a small saucepan. Heat on medium, stirring / lightly mashing raspberries, cooking until sugar is completely dissolved. Remove from heat and cool.

Chill cooled cheesecake thoroughly before serving, serve slices with raspberry sauce.

Peachy Southern Comfort Cheesecake

Crust:

Finely chopped pecans	1 ½ cup	375 ml
Sugar	1/4 cup	50 ml
Butter, melted	5 Tbsp	75 ml

Combine all ingredients until completely incorporated & moistened. Evenly distribute across the bottom of a 9" spring form pan. Press ingredients firmly, extending crust partway up the sides of the pan. Chill for at least 1 hour.

Filling:

Cream cheese, room temperature	2 lbs	1000g
Sugar	1 ½ cups	375 ml
Sour cream	1 cup	250 ml
Heavy cream	½ cup	125 ml
Southern Comfort	1/4 cup	50 ml
Eggs	6	6
Juice of one lemon		

Topping:

Peaches, sliced	4	4
Sugar	1 cup	250 ml
Southern Comfort	1 cup	250 ml

Preheat oven to 425°F (220°C)

In stand mixer, beat together cream cheese and sugar until smooth. Add sour cream, heavy cream, Southern Comfort, eggs, and lemon juice. Beat on low / medium-low until smooth.

Gently pour batter into prepared crust. Chill for 10 minutes.

Bake for 15 minutes. After 15 minutes, turn the oven down to 325°F (160°C) and bake for 50 minutes. Once baking time is complete, turn off the oven and allow cake to cool - WITHOUT opening the door! - for 2 hours.

Meanwhile, combine sugar and Southern Comfort in a medium saucepan. Bring to a boil, stirring often. Turn heat to medium low, add in peach slices. Cook, stirring often, for 15-20 minutes, or until peaches are desired firmness. Remove peaches with a slotted spoon, reserve. Return syrup to stove and simmer until quite thick, stirring constantly.

Top cheesecake with sliced peaches, and chill thoroughly before serving. Serve with Southern Comfort syrup.

Peachy Southern Comfort Cheesecake

Pina Colada Cheesecake

Crust:

Graham cracker crumbs	1 cup	250 ml
Finely chopped macadamia nuts	½ cup	125 ml
Sugar	1/4 cup	50 ml
Butter, melted	5 Tbsp	75 ml

Combine all ingredients until completely incorporated & moistened. Evenly distribute across the bottom of a 9" springform pan. Press ingredients firmly, extending crust partway up the sides of the pan. Chill for at least 1 hour.

Filling:

Cream cheese, room temperature	2 lbs	1000 g
Sugar	1 ½ cups	375 ml
Sour cream	½ cup	125 ml
Very thick pina colada mix	½ cup	125 ml
Creamed coconut	½ cup	125 ml
Rum	½ cup	125 ml
Eggs	6	6
juice of one lemon		

Sauce:

Pineapple juice	1/3 cup	75 ml
Rum	1/3 cup	75 ml
Sugar	1 1/3 cup	325 ml

Toasted coconut, optional

Preheat oven to 425°F (220°C)

In stand mixer, beat together cream cheese and sugar until smooth. Add sour cream, pina colada mix, creamed coconut, rum, eggs, and lemon juice. Beat on low / medium-low until smooth. Gently pour batter into prepared crust. Chill for 10 minutes.

Bake for 15 minutes. After 15 minutes, turn the oven down to 325°F (160°C) and bake for 50 minutes. Once baking time is complete, turn off the oven and allow cake to cool - WITHOUT opening the door! - for 2 hours.

Meanwhile, combine pineapple juice, rum and sugar in medium saucepan. Cook on medium, stirring often, until all sugar is dissolved. Continue simmering until syrup reaches desired thickness. Remove from heat and allow to cool.

Chill cheesecake thoroughly before serving. Drizzle slices with pineapple rum sauce, garnish with toasted coconut, if desired.

Grasshopper Cheesecake

Crust:

Chocolate cookie crumbs	1 ½ cups	375 ml
Sugar	1/4 cup	50 ml
Butter, melted	5 Tbsp	75 ml

Combine all ingredients until completely incorporated & moistened. Evenly distribute across the bottom of a 9" spring form pan. Press ingredients firmly, extending crust partway up the sides of the pan. Chill for at least 1 hour.

Filling:

Cream cheese, room temperature	2 lbs	1000 g
Sugar	1 ½ cups	375 ml
Sour cream	3/4 cup	175 ml
Heavy cream	½ cup	125 ml
Green creme de menthe	½ cup	125 ml
Eggs	6	6
Juice of one lemon		
Andes mint chips	½ cup	125 ml

Chocolate- Mint Sauce:

1 cup Andes Mint chips	1 cup	250 ml
½ cup heavy cream	½ cup	125 ml

Preheat oven to 425°F (220°C).

In stand mixer, beat together cream cheese and sugar until smooth. Add sour cream, heavy cream, creme de menthe, eggs, and lemon juice. Beat on low / medium-low until smooth. Stir in Andes mint chips, gently pour batter into prepared crust. Chill for 10 minutes.

Bake for 15 minutes. After 15 minutes, turn the oven down to 325°F (160°C) and bake for 50 minutes. Once baking time is complete, turn off the oven and allow cake to cool - WITHOUT opening the door! - for 2 hours.

Meanwhile, heat heavy cream to a boil. In a glass bowl, pour over Andes mint chips. Let sit for about 5 minutes, then stir until chips are melted and mixture is smooth. Allow to cool to room temperature.

Chill cheesecake before serving. Drizzle slices with chocolate mint sauce.

Pastry Cream

Pastry Cream - also known as crème pâtissière - is a very thick, rich custard. It's used in many French pastries- such as Eclairs (page 118!)- and also as filling for tarts and cakes. These recipes make about 1 cup of finished pastry cream each - feel free to double or triple the recipe if needed.

Cream Liqueur Pastry Cream

Large egg yolks	3	3
Sugar	1/4 cup	50 ml
Flour	1 ½ Tbsp	25 ml
Cream liqueur of choice.	½ cup	125 ml
Milk	½ cup	125ml
Butter	2 Tbsp	30 ml

Whisk yolks together with sugar until fluffy and pale yellow. Add flour, whisk until incorporated and smooth. Set aside.

In a small saucepan, bring liqueur and milk to a light boil.

Measure about 1/4 cup (50 ml)of the hot milk liquid, and stream slowly into egg mixture while whisking. Continue streaming liquid and whisking until it is completely incorporated, and mixture is smooth. Repeat with another 1/4 cup (50 ml) of hot liquid.

Remove saucepan from heat, pour egg mixture into milk mixture, whisking constantly. Once fully incorporated and smooth, return to heat. Turn heat down to low.

Continue whisking mixture constantly, cooking until mixture is very thick. Remove from heat, whisk in butter until fully incorporated and smooth. Cover with plastic wrap, chill until needed.

Chocolate & Cream Liqueur Pastry Cream

Large egg yolks	3	3
Sugar	1/4 cup	50 ml
Flour	1 ½ Tbsp	25 ml
Cream liqueur of choice.	½ cup	125 ml
Milk	½ cup	125ml
Butter	2 Tbsp	30 ml
Chocolate of choice, melted	3 oz	85 g

Whisk yolks together with sugar until fluffy and pale yellow. Add flour, whisk until incorporated and smooth. Set aside.

In a small saucepan, bring liqueur and milk to a light boil.

Measure about 1/4 cup (50 ml) of the hot milk mixture, and stream slowly into egg mixture while whisking. Continue streaming liquid and whisking until it is completely incorporated, and mixture is smooth. Repeat with another 1/4 cup (50 ml) of hot liquid.

Remove saucepan from heat, pour egg mixture into milk mixture, whisking constantly. Once fully incorporated and smooth, return to heat. Turn heat down to low.

Continue whisking mixture constantly, cooking until mixture is very thick. Remove from heat, whisk in butter until fully incorporated and smooth. Add in melted chocolate, combine until fully incorporated and smooth.

Cover with plastic wrap, chill until needed.

Flavor combination ideas:

Amarula & Dark Chocolate   *   Godiva & any chocolate

Tequila Rose & Milk Chocolate   *   Starbuck's Cream Liqueur & Dark Chocolate

Chai Liqueur & White Chocolate   *   Baja Luna & White Chocolate

Dooley's & Milk Chocolate   *   Bailey's & Milk Chocolate

Non-Cream Liqueur Pastry Cream

Large egg yolks	3	3
Sugar	1/4 cup	50 ml
Flour	1 ½ Tbsp	25 ml
Cream liqueur of choice.	½ cup	125 ml
Heavy cream	½ cup	125ml
Butter	2 Tbsp	30 ml

Whisk yolks together with sugar until fluffy and pale yellow. Add flour, whisk until incorporated and smooth. Set aside.

In a small saucepan, bring liqueur and heavy cream to a light boil.

Measure about 1/4 cup (50 ml) of the hot cream mixture, and stream slowly into egg mixture while whisking. Continue streaming liquid and whisking until it is completely incorporated, and mixture is smooth. Repeat with another 1/4 cup (50 ml) of hot liquid.

Remove saucepan from heat, pour egg mixture into cream mixture, whisking constantly. Once fully incorporated and smooth, return to heat. Turn heat down to low.

Continue whisking mixture constantly, cooking until mixture is very thick. Remove from heat, whisk in butter until fully incorporated and smooth. Cover with plastic wrap, chill until needed.

Chocolate and Non-Cream Liqueur Pastry Cream

Large egg yolks	3	3
Sugar	1/4 cup	50 ml
Flour	1 ½ Tbsp	25 ml
Cream liqueur of choice.	½ cup	125 ml
Heavy cream	½ cup	125ml
Butter	2 Tbsp	30 ml
Chocolate of choice, melted	3 oz	85 g

Whisk yolks together with sugar until fluffy and pale yellow. Add flour, whisk until incorporated and smooth. Set aside.

In a small saucepan, bring liqueur and heavy cream to a light boil.

Measure about 1/4 cup (50 ml) of the hot cream liquid, and stream slowly into egg mixture while whisking. Continue streaming liquid and whisking until it is completely incorporated, and mixture is smooth. Repeat with another 1/4 cup (50 ml) of hot liquid.

Remove saucepan from heat, pour egg mixture into cream mixture, whisking constantly. Once fully incorporated and smooth, return to heat. Turn heat down to low.

Continue whisking mixture constantly, cooking until mixture is very thick. Remove from heat, whisk in butter until fully incorporated and smooth. Add in melted chocolate, combine until fully incorporated and smooth.

Cover with plastic wrap, chill until needed

Flavor combination ideas:

Grand Marnier & Dark Chocolate   *   Limoncello & White Chocolate
PAMA & White Chocolate * Creme De Menthe & Dark Chocolate
Creme De Banane & Milk Chocolate * Jägermeister & Dark Chocolate
Midori & Creme De Banane (1/4 cup / 50 ml each), & White Chocolate

Puddings

Basic Boozy Pudding

Whole milk	2 ½ cups	625 ml
Sugar	½ cup	125 ml
Liqueur of choice	½ cup	125 ml
Cornstarch	1/4 cup	50 ml
Salt	1/8 tsp	½ ml
Butter	2 Tbsp	30 ml

Combine 2 cups (500 ml) of the milk with sugar in a saucepan. Heat to just to a simmer, stirring occasionally.

Meanwhile, whisk together remaining milk, liqueur, cornstarch, and salt until smooth. Pour into the hot milk, whisking constantly to incorporate. Continue to whisk over medium heat until mixture is thick, and coats the back of a spoon, being careful to not allow it to boil.

Remove from heat, stir in butter, and pour into serving dishes. Chill completely before serving.

Basic Boozy Chocolate Pudding

Whole milk	2 ½ cups	625 ml
Liqueur of choice	½ cup	125 ml
Cornstarch	1/4 cup	50 ml
Sugar	½ cup	125 ml
Salt	1/8 tsp	½ ml
Butter	2 Tbsp	30 ml
Chocolate of choice, melted	8 oz	250 g

Combine 2 cups (500 ml) of the milk with sugar in a saucepan. Heat to just to a simmer, stirring occasionally.

Meanwhile, whisk together remaining milk, liqueur, cornstarch, and salt until smooth. Pour into the hot milk, whisking constantly to incorporate. Continue to whisk over medium heat until mixture is thick, and coats the back of a spoon, being careful to not allow it to boil.

Remove from heat, stir in butter and melted chocolate. Pour into serving dishes, and chill completely before serving.

Orange Cream Tequila Pudding

Panna Cotta

Basic Boozy Panna Cotta

Unflavored gelatin powder	1 ½ tsp	7 ml
Cold water	3 Tbsp	15 ml
Milk	1/2 cup	125 ml
Heavy cream	1 cup	250 ml
Sugar	½ cup	125 ml
Liqueur of choice	1/4 cup	50 ml
Sour cream	½ cup	125 ml

Sprinkle the gelatin over the cold water in a small bowl and let absorb for five minutes.

Combine milk, heavy cream, and sugar in a saucepan. Heat to just to a simmer, stirring occasionally. Do not let it come to boil! Meanwhile, microwave the gelatin for about 15 seconds, or until it's melted.   Once the milk mixture has come to a simmer, remove it from the heat. Whisk in the gelatin until fully incorporated, and the mixture is smooth. Add liqueur and sour cream, whisking once again till fully incorporated and smooth. Pour into four greased ramekins or custard cups. Chill for at least 2 hours until set.

Flavor ideas: Almost any liqueur will work with this recipe - experiment with your favorites!

Kahlua Panna Cotta

Basic Boozy Chocolate Panna Cotta

Unflavored gelatin powder	1 ½ tsp	7 ml
Cold water	3 Tbsp	15 ml
Heavy cream	1 ½ cup	375 ml
Sugar	½ cup	125 ml
Chocolate of choice, chopped	4 oz	125 g
Liqueur of choice	1/4 cup	50 ml
Sour Cream	½ cup	125 ml

Sprinkle the gelatin over the cold water in a small bowl and let absorb for five minutes.

Combine heavy cream, and sugar in a saucepan. Heat to just to a simmer, stirring occasionally. Do not let it come to boil! Remove from heat, add chocolate, and stir until chocolate is melted and fully incorporated. Meanwhile, microwave the gelatin for about 15 seconds, or until it's melted.

Whisk the gelatin into the chocolate mixture until fully incorporated, and smooth. Add liqueur and sour cream, whisking once again till fully incorporated and smooth. Pour into four greased ramekins or custard cups. Chill for at least 2 hours until set.

Flavor ideas: See lists under chocolate pastry cream recipes

Basic Boozy, Fruity Panna Cotta

Unflavored gelatin powder	1 ½ tsp	7 ml
Cold water	3 Tbsp	15 ml
Fruit Juice of choice	1 cup	250 ml
Heavy cream	1 cup	250 ml
Sugar	½ cup	125 ml
Liqueur of choice	1/4 cup	50 ml
Sour Cream	½ cup	125 ml

Sprinkle the gelatin over the cold water in a small bowl and let absorb for five minutes.

In a small saucepan, heat fruit juice to boiling. Boil till reduced by half, about 5 minutes. Remove from heat, set aside.

Combine heavy cream and sugar in a saucepan. Heat to just to a simmer, stirring occasionally. Do not let it come to boil! Meanwhile, microwave the gelatin for about 15 seconds, or until it's melted.

Once the cream mixture has come to a simmer, remove it from the heat. Whisk in the gelatin until fully incorporated, and the mixture is smooth. Add fruit juice, stirring until smooth. Add liqueur and sour cream, whisking once again till fully incorporated and smooth. Pour into four greased ramekins or custard cups. Chill for at least 2 hours until set.

* Freshly squeezed juice works best, but you can use bottled/canned also.

Flavor ideas:

- Any tropical fruit with rum
- Any tropical fruit with tequila
- Orange juice with triple sec
- Lemon juice with whisky
- Apple juice with brandy
- Cranberry juice & Grand Marnier
- Orange juice & peach schnapps
- Cranberry juice & sour apple schnapps.

Have fun with it!

(Pictured: Mango puree - rather than juice - with rum. A mango daiquiri panna cotta!)

Mousse

When it comes to mousse, there are two main styles - "Traditional" and "Easy". Traditional mousse is made with raw egg yolks and/or egg whites. While this is perfectly safe for the vast majority of the population, pregnant women, the elderly, and immune compromised individuals may want to opt for the Easy version, which does not contain any raw eggs. Almost any liqueur will work with these recipes - have fun with it! My personal favorites are dark chocolate with walnut cream liqueur, & milk chocolate with strawberry cream tequila. When it comes to the fruit mousse, you can't go wrong with a mango/rum combination.. strawberries with Grand Marnier... cherries and brandy... pears with mead... yum!

Basic Boozy Mousse (Easy)

Unflavored gelatin powder	1 ½ tsp	7 ml
Liqueur of choice	1/3 cup	75 ml
Sugar	1/3 cup	75 ml
Heavy cream	2 cups	500 ml

In a small bowl, sprinkle gelatin over liqueur and allow to soak for 5 minutes. Transfer bowl to microwave, heat in 10 second increments until gelatin dissolves into the liqueur.

Combine sugar and heavy cream together in a mixing bowl. Whip until stiff peaks form, then carefully fold in the liqueur and gelatin mixture, stirring until combined. Pour into 6-8 serving glasses, chill until set, about 2 hours.

Basic Boozy Chocolate Mousse (Easy)

Chocolate	12 ounces	340 g
Butter	4 Tbsp	60 ml
Heavy cream	1 3/4 cups	425 ml
Unflavored gelatin powder	1 tsp	5 ml
Liqueur of choice	1/3 cup	75 ml

Combine chocolate, butter, and heavy cream in the top of a double boiler. Melt together over simmering water, stirring until smooth. Cool to room temperature, then chill until cold.

In a small bowl, sprinkle gelatin over liqueur and allow to soak for 5 minutes. Transfer bowl to microwave, heat in 10 second increments until gelatin dissolves into the liqueur.

Whip chilled chocolate mixture until stiff peaks form, then carefully fold in the liqueur and gelatin mixture, stirring until combined. Pour into 6-8 serving glasses, chill until set, about 2 hours.

Basic Boozy Mousse (Traditional)

Sugar	1/4 cup	50 ml
Egg yolks	2	2
Heavy cream	3/4 cup	175 ml
Liqueur of choice	1/4 cup	50 ml
Egg whites	3	3

Combine sugar and egg yolks together, beat until pale yellow and fluffy. Stir in heavy cream and liqueur a little at a time, until fully incorporated. Whip until stiff peaks form, transfer to fridge.

In a separate bowl, whip the egg whites until stiff peaks form. Carefully fold in chilled whipped cream mixture, stirring until combined. Pour into 4-6 serving glasses, chill until set, about 2 hours.

Basic Boozy Fruit Mousse

Fruit puree *	1 cup	250 ml
Sugar	1/4 cup	50 ml
Unflavored gelatin powder	3 tsp	15 ml
Liqueur of choice	1/3 cup	75 ml
Large egg whites	2	2
Heavy cream	1 cup	250 ml

Combine fruit puree and sugar together in a large bowl, set aside.

In a small bowl, sprinkle gelatin over liqueur and allow to soak for 5 minutes. Transfer bowl to microwave, heat in 10 second increments until gelatin dissolves into the liqueur. Pour into fruit puree mixture, stir until well incorporated, then chill while preparing the rest of the ingredients. In a separate bowl, whip egg whites until stiff peaks form. Carefully fold into chilled fruit mixture, stirring until combined.

Whip cream until stiff peaks form, then carefully fold in to the fruit mixture, stirring until combined. Pour into 6-8 serving glasses, chill until set, about 2 hours.

* If you have access to pre made fruit puree, that is easiest. Certain fruits - such as berries - puree well without any cooking. More firm fruits, such as pears, should be chopped and cooked until soft before pureeing. If you want to be really quick and dirty about it, you can puree canned fruit - strain the liquid off first!

Certain fruits - such as pineapple, papaya, and kiwi fruit - contain enzymes that break down the protein strands in gelatin. It is important to thoroughly cook these fruits before using them in this recipe. Another alternative would be to use canned, as they are pre-cooked.

Raspberry Mousse with Grand Marnier

Basic Boozy Chocolate Mousse (Traditional)

Chocolate of choice	4 ½ oz	140 g
Butter	2 Tbsp	30 ml
Liqueur of choice	2 Tbsp	30 ml
Heavy cream	1 cup	250 ml
Large eggs, separated	3	3
Sugar	1 Tbsp	15 ml

Combine chocolate, butter, liqueur, and heavy cream in the top of a double boiler. Melt together over simmering water, stirring until smooth. Cool to almost room temperature.

Combine sugar and egg yolks together, beat until pale yellow and fluffy. Stir in chocolate mixture a little at a time, until fully incorporated. Transfer to fridge, chill completely.

Whip chilled chocolate mixture until stiff peaks form. In a separate bowl, whip the egg whites until stiff peaks form. Carefully fold in chilled chocolate mixture, stirring until combined. Pour into 4-6 serving glasses, chill until set, about 2 hours.

Chiffon Pies

Basic Boozy Chiffon Pie

Crumb pie crust (Page 27)	1	1
Unflavored Gelatin powder	1 ½ tsp	7 ml
Liqueur of choice	½ cup	125 ml
Sugar	½ cup	125 ml
Egg yolks	3	3
Heavy cream	2 cups	500 ml

Following cheesecake crust recipe, prepare crust. Press into bottom and sides of a pie plate, chill for 30 minutes.

In a small bowl, sprinkle gelatin over liqueur and allow to soak for 5 minutes. Transfer bowl to microwave, heat in 10 second increments until gelatin dissolves into the liqueur.

Combine sugar and egg yolks together, beat until pale yellow and fluffy. Stir in liqueur mixture a little at a time, until fully incorporated.

In a separate bowl, whip heavy cream until stiff peaks form. Carefully fold in the liqueur, egg, and gelatin mixture, stirring until combined. Pour into pie crust, chill until set - at least 6 hours, preferably overnight.

Basic Boozy Fruit Chiffon Pie

Crumb pie crust (Cheesecake section)	1	1
Fruit puree *	1 cup	250 ml
Sugar	1/4 cup	50 ml
Unflavored gelatin powder	3 tsp	15 ml
Liqueur of choice	1/3 cup	75 ml
Large egg whites	2	2
Heavy cream	1 cup	250 ml

Following cheesecake crust recipe, prepare crust. Press into bottom and sides of a pie plate, chill for 30 minutes.

Combine fruit puree and sugar together in a large bowl, set aside.

In a small bowl, sprinkle gelatin over liqueur and allow to soak for 5 minutes. Transfer bowl to microwave, heat in 10 second increments until gelatin dissolves into the liqueur. Pour into fruit puree mixture, stir until well incorporated, then chill.

In a separate bowl, whip egg whites until stiff peaks form. Carefully fold into chilled fruit mixture, stirring until combined.

Whip cream until stiff peaks form, then carefully fold in to the fruit mixture, stirring until combined. Pour into pie crust, chill until set - at least 6 hours, preferably overnight.

* If you have access to pre made fruit puree, that is easiest. Certain fruits - such as berries - puree well without any cooking. More firm fruits, such as pears, should be chopped and cooked until soft before pureeing. If you want to be really quick and dirty about it, you can puree canned fruit - strain the liquid off first!

Certain fruits - such as pineapple, papaya, and kiwi fruit - contain enzymes that break down the protein strands in gelatin. It is important to thoroughly cook these fruits before using them in this recipe. Another alternative would be to use canned, as they are pre-cooked.

A few flavoring ideas:

- Strawberry Daiquiri - Use strawberries for the puree. Add 1 tbsp (15 ml) lime juice and 2 tsp (10 ml) freshly grated lime zest, with rum in place of the liqueur.

- Lime Margarita: Increase sugar to ½ cup (125 ml). Replace fruit puree with ½ cup (125 ml) lime juice, and 2 tsp (10 ml) freshly grated lime zest, use tequila for the liqueur. (Rum for a daiquiri)

- Lemon Drop: Increase sugar to ½ cup (125 ml). Replace fruit puree with ½ cup (125 ml) lemon juice, and 2 tsp (10 ml) freshly grated lemon zest, use vodka in place of the liqueur.

- Tropical: Use a macadamia nut crust, pineapple puree , and rum for the liqueur!

- Fuzzy Navel: Use ½ cup (125 ml) peach puree and ½ cup (125 ml) orange juice in place of puree, and peach schnapps for the liqueur

- Cosmo: Increase sugar to ½ cup (125 ml). Use ½ cup (125 ml) cooked cranberry puree and ½ cup (125 ml) cranberry juice. Add 1 tbsp (15 ml) lime juice and 2 tsp (10 ml) freshly grated lime zest, with Grand Marnier for the liqueur

Grasshopper Pie

Oreo pie crust (Cheesecake section)	1	1
Unflavored gelatin powder	1 ½ tsp	7 ml
Green creme de menthe	1/4 cup	50 ml
White creme de cacao	1/4 cup	50 ml
Sugar	½ cup	125 ml
Egg yolks	3	3
Heavy cream	2 cups	500 ml

Following cheesecake crust recipe, prepare crust. Press into bottom and sides of a pie plate, chill for 30 minutes.

In a small bowl, sprinkle gelatin over liqueurs and allow to soak for 5 minutes. Transfer bowl to microwave, heat in 10 second increments until gelatin dissolves into the liqueur.

Combine sugar and egg yolks together, beat until pale yellow and fluffy. Stir in liqueur mixture a little at a time, until fully incorporated.

In a separate bowl, whip heavy cream until stiff peaks form. Carefully fold in the liqueur, egg, and gelatin mixture, stirring until combined. Pour into pie crust, chill until set - at least 6 hours, preferably overnight.

Fondue

There are few things as tempting as a fondue. Humans have a deep seeded urge to dip their food into stuff. When "food" refers to fruit and cake, and "stuff" is melted chocolate, all the better!

Boozy Dark Chocolate Fondue

Dark chocolate	12 oz	340 g
Heavy cream	1 cup	250 ml
Liqueur of choice, warmed	1/4 cup	50 ml

Coarsely chop chocolate, combine with cream in saucepan. Melt chocolate over very low heat, stirring until combined and smooth. Stir in liqueur of choice, transfer to fondue pot. Serve with fruit, cubes of pound cake, cookies, marshmallows, and anything else you like!

Boozy Milk Chocolate Fondue

Milk chocolate	12 oz	340 g
Heavy cream	3/4 cup	175 ml
Liqueur of choice , warmed	1/4 cup	50 ml

Coarsely chop chocolate, combine with cream in saucepan. Melt chocolate over very low heat, stirring until combined and smooth. Stir in liqueur of choice, transfer to fondue pot. Serve with fruit, cubes of pound cake, marshmallows, and anything else you like!

Boozy White Chocolate Fondue

Dark chocolate	12 oz	340 g
Heavy cream	½ cup	125 ml
Liqueur of choice	1/4 cup	50 ml

Coarsely chop chocolate, combine with cream in saucepan. Melt chocolate over very low heat, stirring until combined and smooth. Stir in liqueur of choice, transfer to fondue pot. Serve with fruit, cubes of pound cake, marshmallows, and anything else you like!

Boozy Tropical Coconut Fondue

Coconut cream	1 cup	250 ml
Cornstarch	4 tsp	20 ml
Unsweetened coconut milk	2 cups	500 ml
Sugar	3 Tbsp	45 ml
Amber or dark rum	3/4 cup	175 ml

Combine coconut cream and cornstarch, whisking until smooth with no lumps. Combine with coconut milk and sugar in a medium saucepan. Heat to boiling, reduce heat, and simmer for 10 minutes, or until thickened. Remove from heat, stir in rum, transfer to fondue pot.

Serve with cubes of mango, pineapple, kiwi, papaya, cookies, and anything else you'd like. A bowl of toasted coconut to roll dipped fruit in is a nice touch, as well!

Boozy Citrus Fondue

Egg yolks	8	8
Sugar	½ cup	125 ml
Freshly squeezed juice*	1 cup	250 ml
Liqueur of choice**	1/4 cup	50 ml

In a stainless steel bowl placed over a saucepan of simmering water, whisk together the eggs, sugar, and juice until blended. Cook, stirring constantly, until mixture is thick, fluffy, and coats the back of a spoon. Remove from heat, stir in liqueur, transfer to fondue pot.

Serve with fruit, cubes of pound cake, marshmallows, and anything else you like!

* Feel free to use any citrus fruit for the juice - orange, lemon, lime, grapefruit... or any combination of them! While store bought juice will work, freshly squeezed really does taste better.

** While any non-cream based liqueur will work in this, I recommend citrusy liqueurs like Triple Sec, Grand Marnier, or even lemon infused vodka.

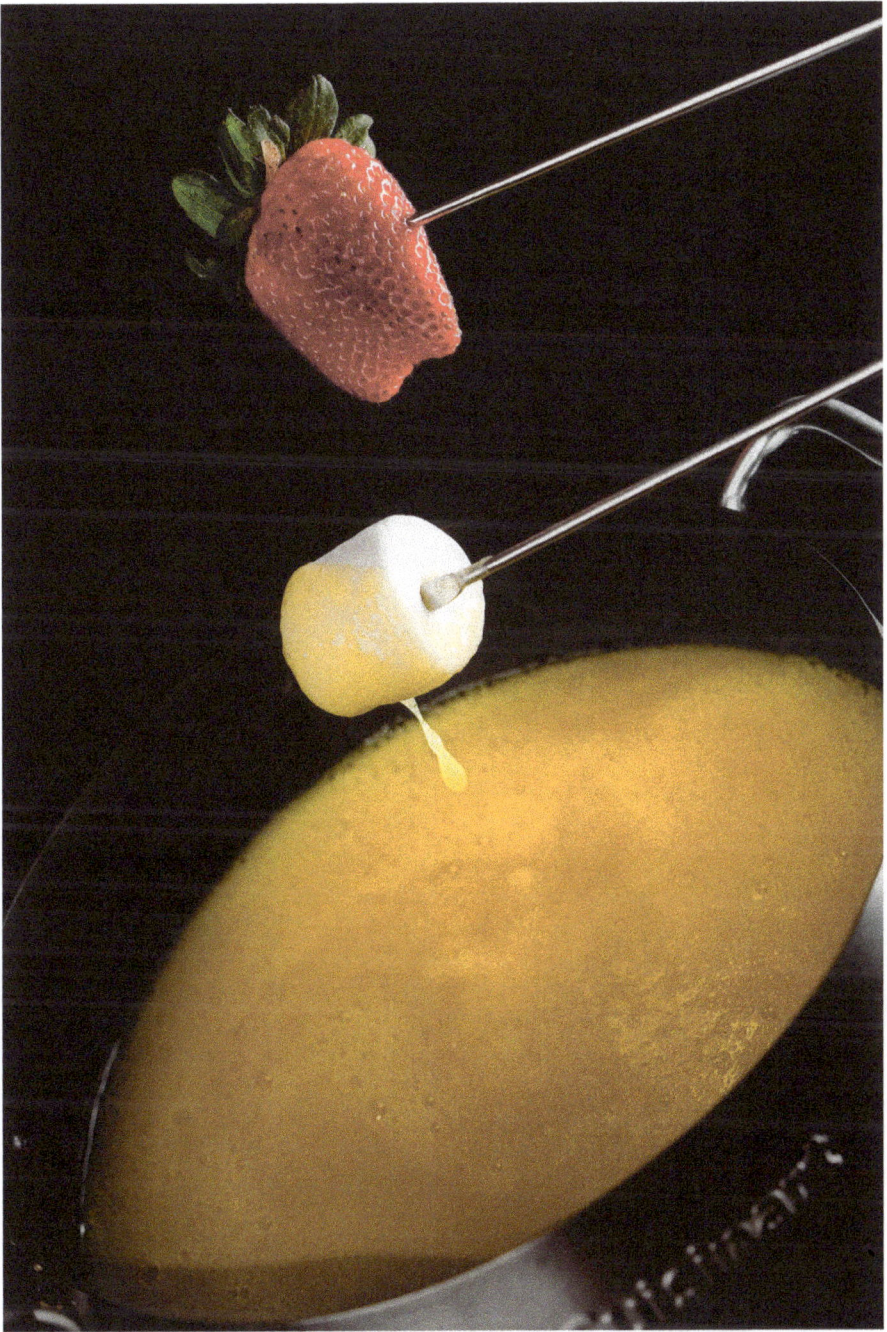

Boozy Citrus Fondue

Boozy Cheesecake Fondue

Cream cheese	8 oz	250 g
Heavy cream	1/4 cup	50 ml
Sugar	1/4 cup	50 ml
Liqueur of choice	1/4 cup	50 ml

Heat cream cheese until soft, combine with cream in saucepan. Stir over medium heat until cream cheese is melted and fully incorporated into the cream. Add sugar. Cook for 2 minutes, stirring frequently, until sugar is dissolved. Stir in liqueur of choice, transfer to fondue pot.

Serve with fruit, cubes of pound cake, marshmallows, and anything else you like!

Boozy Caramel Fondue

Sugar	2 cups	500 ml
Corn syrup	½ cup	125 ml
Water	1/4 cup	50 ml
Heavy Cream	1 cup	250 ml
Liqueur of choice	½ cup	125 ml
Butter	½ cup	125 ml

Combine sugar, corn syrup, and water in a medium sauce pan. Cook over low heat, stirring until sugar dissolves, 5-7 minutes.

Increase heat to medium and simmer until syrup turns to a deep golden brown, stirring often and occasionally brushing down the sides of the saucepan with a wet brush. This will take about 25-35 minutes.

Remove from heat, carefully add cream, liqueur, and butter. Stir until butter is melted, and everything is incorporated and smooth. Allow caramel to cool for at least 30 minutes, stirring occasionally. Transfer to fondue pot.

Serve with fruit, cubes of pound cake, cookies, marshmallows, and anything else you like!

Basic Boozy Flan

Once again, here is a base recipe that almost any liqueur will work well with, so have fun with it! Kahlua is a popular choice, but my personal favorite is a "Candy Apple" flan! To make it, use 1/2 cup (125 ml) each of apple flavored vodka and sour apple schnapps for the liqueur.. and
add a little green food coloring!

Sugar	2 cups	500 ml
Water	1/4 cup	50 ml
Large eggs	10	10
Sugar	1/2 cup	125 ml
Liqueur of choice	1 cup	250 ml
Heavy cream	2 cups	500 ml
Milk	1 cup	250 ml
Cocoa, optional*	1/4 cup	50 ml

Preheat oven to 350°F (180°C)

Combine 2 cups (500 ml)of the sugar with water in a small saucepan over medium heat. Stir until sugar is a light golden brown, about 15 - 20 minutes. Pour into generously greased flan pan, quiche dish or glass baking dish.

Combine eggs, sugar, and liqueur, beat until well blended and smooth. Add heavy cream and milk, stir until fully incorporated. Slowly and carefully pour over the caramel in the flan pan.

Place flan pan into a larger baking pan. Carefully add water to the large pan, till about halfway up the sides of the flan pan. Bake for 45 - 60 minutes or until custard is set. Cool to room temperature, then chill completely.

To serve, run a knife around the outside edge of the flan to loosen. Place a serving plate - face down - over the baking dish, and carefully invert.

* If using cocoa, beat into eggs, sugar, and liqueur mixture, before adding cream and milk.

Crème Brûlée

Basic Boozy Crème Brûlée

Egg yolks	8	8
Sugar	1/4 cup	50 ml
Cream liqueur of choice	½ cup	125 ml
Heavy cream	1 ½ cups	375 ml
Sugar	1/4 cup	50 ml

Preheat oven to 325°F (160°C)

Combine egg yolks and sugar together in a bowl, whisking until the mixture becomes thick and pale yellow. Add approximately half of the liqueur, whisking until incorporated and smooth.

In a small saucepan, combine remaining liqueur with heavy cream, heating to a simmer. Remove from heat. Slowly drizzle hot cream mixture into the egg mixture, whisking constantly. Pour into 6 ramekins or custard cups, and arrange in a large pan. Carefully add water to the large pan, till about halfway up the sides of the ramekins.

Bake until custard is set, but wiggles in the middle - about 45-50 minutes. Remove from oven, allow to cool to room temperature, and then chill
for at least 2 hours.

When ready to serve, sprinkle 2-3 tsp (10-15 ml) sugar evenly over each custard. Use a small, hand held kitchen torch to melt sugar.

Flavor ideas: This works well with any cream based liqueur, so go with what you love. My favorites are Amarula and Baja Rosa.

Basic Boozy Crème Brûlée

Basic Boozy Chocolate Crème Brûlée

Egg yolks	8	8
Sugar	1/4 cup	50 ml
Cream liqueur of choice	½ cup	125 ml
Heavy cream	1 ½ cups	375 ml
Sugar	1/4 cup	50 ml
Chocolate of choice	4-6 oz	125-170 g

Preheat oven to 325ºF (160°C)

Combine egg yolks and sugar together in a bowl, whisking until mixture becomes thick and pale yellow. Add approximately half of the liqueur, whisking until incorporated and smooth.

In a small saucepan, combine remaining liqueur with heavy cream, heating to a simmer. Remove from heat, add in chocolate, stirring until melted, incorporated, and smooth. Slowly drizzle hot cream mixture into the egg mixture, whisking constantly. Pour into 6 ramekins or custard cups, and arrange in a large pan. Carefully add water to the large pan, till about halfway up the sides of the ramekins.

Bake until custard is set, but wiggles in the middle - about 45-50 minutes. Remove from oven, allow to cool to room temperature, and then chill for at least 2 hours.

When ready to serve, sprinkle 2-3 tsp (10-15 ml) sugar evenly over each custard. Use a small, hand held kitchen torch to melt sugar.

Flavor ideas:

Amarula & dark chocolate * Godiva & any chocolate

Tequila Rose & milk chocolate * Baja Luna & white chocolate

Bailey's & milk chocolate * Dooley's & milk chocolate

Starbuck's cream liqueur & dark chocolate

Chai Liqueur & white chocolate

Cakey

Rum Cakes

Rum cake is the quintessential use of alcohol in baking. These cakes are simple to make, extremely moist, and are always a hit! I call for cake flour in these recipes, but regular all purpose flour may be substituted in a pinch.

Basic Rum Cake

Cake flour	2 cups	500 ml
Sugar	1 ½ cups	375 ml
Baking powder	4 tsp	20 ml
Salt	1 tsp	5 ml
Instant vanilla pudding mix	3 ½ oz	96 g
Large eggs	4	4
Water	½ cup	125 ml
Amber rum	½ cup	125 ml
Butter, melted	1 cup	250 ml
Pecans or walnuts, chopped	1 cup	250 ml

Rum Soak		
Butter	½ cup	125 ml
Water	1/4 cup	50 ml
Sugar	1 cup	250 ml
Amber rum	½ cup	125 ml

Glaze		
Amber rum	1/4 cup	50 ml
Powdered (Icing) sugar	2+ cups	500+ ml

Preheat oven to 325°F (160°C). Generously grease a large (12 cup) Bundt pan with shortening. If using nuts, sprinkle across bottom of greased pan.

Combine flour, sugar, baking powder, salt, and pudding mix in a large mixing bowl. Add in eggs and water, beating until smooth. Carefully add rum and melted butter to the mix, mixing on medium speed until smooth. Pour into prepared Bundt pan and smooth top.

Bake until golden and knife inserted into center of batter comes out clean and cake springs back - about 55 minutes. Remove from oven and place on cooling rack while making soaking glaze.

In a small saucepan combine butter, water and sugar. Heat to a simmer and cook until sugar is dissolved. Remove from heat, carefully add the rum, and mix to combine. While cake is still cooling in the pan, pour hot syrup on top of cake - it may take a few minutes to all soak in. Cool cake in pan for 10 minutes before turning out onto serving platter.

Mix as much icing sugar into the 1/4 cup (50 ml) rum as it takes to make a very thick mix. Melt it in the microwave for a few seconds, then drizzle over the cake.

Chocolate Rum Cake

Cake flour	2 cups	500 ml
Cocoa	1/4 cup	50 ml
Sugar	1 ½ cups	375 ml
Baking powder	4 tsp	20 ml
Salt	1 tsp	5 ml
Instant vanilla pudding mix	3 ½ oz	96 g
Large eggs	4	4
Water	½ cup	125 ml
Dark rum	½ cup	125 ml
Butter, melted	1 cup	250 ml
Pecans or walnuts, chopped	1 cup	250 ml

Rum Soak

Butter	½ cup	125 ml
Water	1/4 cup	50 ml
Sugar	1 cup	250 ml
Dark rum	½ cup	125 ml

Glaze

Dark rum	1/4 cup	50 ml
Powdered (Icing) sugar	2+ cups	500+ ml

Preheat oven to 325°F (160°C). Generously grease a large (12 cup) Bundt pan with shortening. If using nuts, sprinkle across bottom of greased pan.

Combine flour, cocoa, sugar, baking powder, salt, and pudding mix in a large mixing bowl. Add in eggs and water, beating until smooth. Carefully add rum and melted butter to the mix, mixing on medium speed until smooth. Pour into prepared Bundt pan and smooth top. Bake until golden and knife inserted into center of batter comes out clean and cake springs back - about 55 minutes. Remove from oven and place on cooling rack while making soaking glaze.

In a small saucepan combine butter, water and sugar. Heat to a simmer and cook until sugar is dissolved. Remove from heat, carefully add the rum, and mix to combine. While cake is still cooling in the pan, pour hot syrup on top of cake - it may take a few minutes to all soak in. Cool cake in pan for 10 minutes before turning out onto serving platter.

Meanwhile, mix as much icing sugar into the 1/4 cup (50 ml) rum as it takes to make a very thick mix. Melt it in the microwave for a few seconds, then drizzle over the cake.

Coconut Rum Cake

Cake flour	2 cups	500 ml
Coconut	1 cup	250 ml
Sugar	1 ½ cups	375 ml
Baking powder	4 tsp	20 ml
Salt	1 tsp	5 ml
Instant vanilla pudding mix	3 ½ oz	96 g
Large eggs	4	4
Water	½ cup	125 ml
Amber or coconut rum	½ cup	125 ml
Butter, melted	1 cup	250 ml
Pecans or walnuts, chopped	1 cup	250 ml

Rum Soak		
Butter	½ cup	125 ml
Water	1/4 cup	50 ml
Sugar	1 cup	250 ml
Coconut rum	½ cup	125 ml

Glaze		
Amber rum	1/4 cup	50 ml
Powdered (Icing) sugar	2+ cups	500+ ml

Preheat oven to 325°F (160°C). Generously grease a large (12 cup) Bundt pan with shortening. If using nuts, sprinkle across bottom of greased pan.

Combine flour, coconut, sugar, baking powder, salt, and pudding mix in a large mixing bowl. Add in eggs and water, beating until smooth. Carefully add rum and melted butter to the mix, mixing on medium speed until smooth. Pour into prepared Bundt pan and smooth top. Bake until golden and knife inserted into center of batter comes out clean and cake springs back - about 55 minutes. Remove from oven and place on cooling rack while making soaking glaze.

In a small saucepan combine butter, water and sugar. Heat to a simmer and cook until sugar is dissolved. Remove from heat, carefully add the rum, and mix to combine. While cake is still cooling in the pan, pour hot syrup on top of cake - it may take a few minutes to all soak in. Cool cake in pan for 10 minutes before turning out onto serving platter.

Mix as much icing sugar into the 1/4 cup (50 ml) rum as it takes to make a very thick mix. Melt it in the microwave for a few seconds, then drizzle over the cake.

Key Lime Rum Cake

Cake flour	2 cups	500 ml
Sugar	1 ½ cups	375 ml
Baking powder	4 tsp	20 ml
Salt	1 tsp	5 ml
Instant vanilla pudding mix	3 ½ oz	96 g
Large eggs	4	4
Water	1/4 cup	50 ml
Key lime juice	1/4 cup	50 ml
Amber rum	½ cup	125 ml
Butter, melted	1 cup	250 ml

Rum Soak

Butter	½ cup	125 ml
Lime juice	1/4 cup	50 ml
Sugar	1 cup	250 ml
Amber rum	½ cup	125 ml

Glaze

Amber rum	1/4 cup	50 ml
Powdered (Icing) sugar	2+ cups	500+ ml

Preheat oven to 325°F (160°C). Generously grease a large (12 cup) Bundt pan with shortening.

Combine flour, sugar, baking powder, salt, and pudding mix in a large mixing bowl. Add in eggs, water, and lime juice, beating until smooth. Carefully add rum and melted butter to the mix, mixing on medium speed until smooth. Pour into prepared Bundt pan and smooth top.

Bake until golden and knife inserted into center of batter comes out clean and cake springs back - about 55 minutes. Remove from oven and place on cooling rack while making soaking glaze.

In a small saucepan combine butter, lime juice and sugar. Heat to a simmer and cook until sugar is dissolved. Remove from heat, carefully add the rum, and mix to combine. While cake is still cooling in the pan, pour hot syrup on top of cake - it may take a few minutes to all soak in.

Cool cake in pan for 10 minutes before turning out onto serving platter.

Mix as much icing sugar into the 1/4 cup (50 ml) rum as it takes to make a very thick mix. Melt it in the microwave for a few seconds, then drizzle over the cake.

Strawberry Daiquiri Rum Cake

Cake flour	2 cups	500 ml
Sugar	1 ½ cups	375 ml
Baking powder	4 tsp	20 ml
Salt	1 tsp	5 ml
Instant vanilla pudding mix	3 ½ oz	96 g
Large eggs	4	4
Water	1/4 cup	50 ml
Lime juice	2 Tbsp	30 ml
Pureed strawberries	1 cup	250 ml
Amber rum	½ cup	125 ml
Butter, melted	1 cup	250 ml
Pecans or walnuts, chopped	1 cup	250 ml

Rum Soak

Butter	½ cup	125 ml
Water	1/4 cup	50 ml
Sugar	1 cup	250 ml
Amber rum	½ cup	125 ml

Glaze

Amber Rum	1/4 cup	50 ml
Powdered (Icing) sugar	2+ cups	500+ ml

Preheat oven to 325°F (160°C). Generously grease a large (12 cup) Bundt pan with shortening. If using nuts, sprinkle across bottom of greased pan.

Combine flour, sugar, baking powder, salt, and pudding mix in a large mixing bowl. Add in eggs, water, and lime juice, beating until smooth. Carefully add rum and melted butter to the mix, mixing on medium speed until smooth. Stir in pureed strawberries until well incorporated. Pour into prepared Bundt pan and smooth top.

Bake until golden and knife inserted into center of batter comes out clean and cake springs back - about 55 minutes. Remove from oven and place on cooling rack while making soaking glaze.

In a small saucepan combine butter, water and sugar. Heat to a simmer and cook until sugar is dissolved. Remove from heat, carefully add the rum, and mix to combine. While cake is still cooling in the pan, pour hot syrup on top of cake - it may take a few minutes to all soak in. Cool cake in pan for 10 minutes before turning out onto serving platter.

Mix as much icing sugar into the 1/4 cup (50 ml) rum as it takes to make a very thick mix. Melt it in the microwave for a few seconds, then drizzle over the cake.

Pina Colada Rum Cake

Cake flour	2 cups	500 ml
Sugar	1 ½ cups	375 ml
Baking powder	4 tsp	20 ml
Salt	1 tsp	5 ml
Instant vanilla pudding mix	3 ½ oz	96 g
Large eggs	4	4
Pina colada mix	½ cup	125 ml
Amber or dark rum	½ cup	125 ml
Butter, melted	1 cup	250 ml
Crushed pineapple	1 cup	250 ml
Shredded coconut.	1 ½ cups	375 ml

Rum Soak

Butter	½ cup	125 ml
Water	1/4 cup	50 ml
Sugar	1 cup	250 ml
Amber or dark rum	½ cup	125 ml

Glaze

Amber or dark rum	1/4 cup	50 ml
Powdered (Icing) sugar	2+ cups	500+ ml

Preheat oven to 325°F (160°C). Generously grease a large (12 cup) Bundt pan with shortening.

Combine flour, sugar, baking powder, salt, and pudding mix in a large mixing bowl. Add in eggs and pina colada mix, beating until smooth. Carefully add rum and melted butter to the mix, mixing on medium speed until smooth. Add pineapple and coconut, carefully stir by hand until incorporated. Pour into prepared Bundt pan and smooth top.

Bake until golden and knife inserted into center of batter comes out clean and cake springs back - about 55 minutes. Remove from oven and place on cooling rack while making soaking glaze.

In a small saucepan combine butter, water and sugar. Heat to a simmer and cook until sugar is dissolved. Remove from heat, carefully add the rum, and mix to combine. While cake is still cooling in the pan, pour hot syrup on top of cake - it may take a few minutes to all soak in.

Cool cake in pan for 10 minutes before turning out onto serving platter.

Mix as much icing sugar into the 1/4 cup (50 ml) rum as it takes to make a very thick mix. Melt it in the microwave for a few seconds, then drizzle over the cake.

Pina Colada Rum Cake

Cococabana Rum Cake

Cake flour	2 cups	500 ml
Sugar	1 ½ cups	375 ml
Baking powder	4 tsp	20 ml
Salt	1 tsp	5 ml
Instant vanilla pudding mix	3 ½ oz	96 g
Large eggs	4	4
Pineapple juice	½ cup	125 ml
Malibu rum	½ cup	125 ml
Butter, melted	1 cup	250 ml
Shredded coconut	1 cup	250 ml

Rum Soak

Butter	½ cup	125 ml
Water	1/4 cup	50 ml
Sugar	1 cup	250 ml
Melon liqueur	½ cup	125 ml

Glaze

Melon liqueur	1/4 cup	50 ml
Powdered (Icing) sugar	2+ cups	500+ ml

Preheat oven to 325°F (160°C). Generously grease a large (12 cup) Bundt pan with shortening.

Combine flour, sugar, baking powder, salt, and pudding mix in a large mixing bowl. Add in eggs and pineapple juice, beating until smooth. Carefully add rum and melted butter to the mix, mixing on medium speed until smooth. Add coconut, carefully stir by hand until incorporated. Pour into prepared Bundt pan and smooth top.

Bake until golden and knife inserted into center of batter comes out clean and cake springs back - about 55 minutes. Remove from oven and place on cooling rack while making soaking glaze.

In a small saucepan combine butter, water and sugar. Heat to a simmer and cook until sugar is dissolved. Remove from heat, carefully add the melon liqueur, and mix to combine. While cake is still cooling in the pan, pour hot syrup on top of cake - it may take a few minutes to all soak in.

Cool cake in pan for 10 minutes before turning out onto serving platter.

Mix as much icing sugar into the 1/4 cup (50 ml) melon liqueur as it takes to make a very thick mix. Melt it in the microwave for a few seconds, then drizzle over the cake.

Zombie Rum Cake

Cake flour	2 cups	500 ml
Sugar	1 ½ cups	375 ml
Baking powder	4 tsp	20 ml
Salt	1 tsp	5 ml
Instant vanilla pudding mix	3 ½ oz	96 g
Large eggs	4	4
Sweet and sour	1/4 cup	50 ml
Orange juice	1/4 cup	50 ml
Pineapple juice	1/4 cup	50 ml
Amber rum	1/4 cup	50 ml
Butter, melted	1 cup	250 ml

Rum Soak

Butter	½ cup	125 ml
Water	1/4 cup	50 ml
Sugar	1 cup	250 ml
Dark rum	½ cup	125 ml

Glaze

White rum	1/4 cup	50 ml
Powdered (Icing) sugar	2+ cups	500+ ml

Preheat oven to325°F (160°C). Generously grease a large (12 cup) Bundt pan with shortening.

Combine flour, sugar, baking powder, salt, and pudding mix in a large mixing bowl. Add in eggs and sweet and sour, beating until smooth. Carefully add juices, rum and melted butter to the mix, mixing on medium speed until smooth. Pour into prepared Bundt pan and smooth top.

Bake until golden and knife inserted into center of batter comes out clean and cake springs back - about 55 minutes. Remove from oven and place on cooling rack while making soaking glaze.

In a small saucepan combine butter, water and sugar. Heat to a simmer and cook until sugar is dissolved. Remove from heat, carefully add the rum, and mix to combine. While cake is still cooling in the pan, pour hot syrup on top of cake - it may take a few minutes to all soak in.

Cool cake in pan for 10 minutes before turning out onto serving platter.

Mix as much icing sugar into the 1/4 cup (50 ml) rum as it takes to make a very thick mix. Melt it in the microwave for a few seconds, then drizzle over the cake.

Blue Hawaiian Rum Cake

Cake flour	2 cups	500 ml
Sugar	1 ½ cups	375 ml
Baking powder	4 tsp	20 ml
Salt	1 tsp	5 ml
Instant vanilla pudding mix	3 ½ oz	96 g
Large eggs	4	4
Malibu rum	1/3 cup	75 ml
Sweet and sour	1/3 cup	75 ml
Pineapple juice	1/3 cup	75 ml
Butter, melted	1 cup	250 ml

Rum Soak

Butter	½ cup	125 ml
Water	1/4 cup	50 ml
Sugar	1 cup	250 ml
Blue Curacao	½ cup	125 ml

Glaze

Blue Curacao	1/4 cup	50 ml
Powdered (Icing) sugar	2+ cups	500+ ml

Preheat oven to 325°F (160°C). Generously grease a large (12 cup) Bundt pan with shortening.

Combine flour, sugar, baking powder, salt, and pudding mix in a large mixing bowl. Add in eggs and Malibu rum, beating until smooth. Carefully add sweet and sour, pineapple juice, and melted butter to the mix, mixing on medium speed until smooth. Pour into prepared Bundt pan and smooth top.

Bake until golden and knife inserted into center of batter comes out clean and cake springs back - about 55 minutes. Remove from oven and place on cooling rack while making soaking glaze.

In a small saucepan combine butter, water and sugar. Heat to a simmer and cook until sugar is dissolved. Remove from heat, carefully add the Blue Curacao, and mix to combine. While cake is still cooling in the pan, pour hot syrup on top of cake - it may take a few minutes to all soak in.

Cool cake in pan for 10 minutes before turning out onto serving platter.

Mix as much icing sugar into the 1/4 cup (50 ml) Blue Curacao as it takes to make a very thick mix. Melt it in the microwave for a few seconds, then drizzle over the cake.

Blue Hawaiian Rum Cake

Tequila Sunrise Cake

Cake flour	2 cups	500 ml
Sugar	1 ½ cups	375 ml
Baking powder	4 tsp	20 ml
Salt	1 tsp	5 ml
Instant vanilla pudding mix	3 ½ oz	96 g
Large eggs	4	4
Orange juice	½ cup	125 ml
Tequila	½ cup	125 ml
Butter, melted	1 cup	250 ml

Tequila Soak

Butter	½ cup	125 ml
Grenadine	1/4 cup	50 ml
Sugar	½ cup	125 ml
Tequila	½ cup	125 ml

Preheat oven to325°F (160°C). Generously grease a large (12 cup) Bundt pan with shortening.

Combine flour, sugar, baking powder, salt, and pudding mix in a large mixing bowl. Add in eggs and orange juice, beating until smooth. Carefully add tequila and melted butter to the mix, mixing on medium speed until smooth. Pour into prepared Bundt pan and smooth top.

Bake until golden and knife inserted into center of batter comes out clean and cake springs back - about 55 minutes. Remove from oven and place on cooling rack while making soaking glaze.

In a small saucepan combine butter, grenadine and sugar. Heat to a simmer and cook until sugar is dissolved. Remove from heat, carefully add the tequila, and mix to combine. While cake is still cooling in the pan, pour hot syrup on top of cake - it may take a few minutes to all soak in.

Cool cake in pan for 10 minutes before turning out onto serving platter.

Fuzzy Navel Cake

Cake flour	2 cups	500 ml
Sugar	1 ½ cups	375 ml
Baking powder	4 tsp	20 ml
Salt	1 tsp	5 ml
Instant vanilla pudding mix	3 ½ oz	96 g
Large eggs	4	4
Orange juice	3/4 cup	175 ml
Peach schnapps	1/4 cup	50 ml
Butter, melted	1 cup	250 ml

Peach Soak

Butter	½ cup	125 ml
Water	1/4 cup	50 ml
Sugar	1 cup	250 ml
Peach schnapps	½ cup	125 ml

Preheat oven to325°F (160°C). Generously grease a large (12 cup) Bundt pan with shortening.

Combine flour, sugar, baking powder, salt, and pudding mix in a large mixing bowl. Add in eggs and orange juice, beating until smooth. Carefully add peach schnapps and melted butter to the mix, mixing on medium speed until smooth. Pour into prepared Bundt pan and smooth top.

Bake until golden and knife inserted into center of batter comes out clean and cake springs back - about 55 minutes. Remove from oven and place on cooling rack while making soaking glaze.

In a small saucepan combine butter, water and sugar. Heat to a simmer and cook until sugar is dissolved. Remove from heat, carefully add the peach schnapps, and mix to combine. While cake is still cooling in the pan, pour hot syrup on top of cake - it may take a few minutes to all soak in.

Cool cake in pan for 10 minutes before turning out onto serving platter.

Cranberry - Apple Brandy Bundt Cake

Cake flour	2 cups	500 ml
Sugar	1 ½ cups	375 ml
Baking powder	4 tsp	20 ml
Salt	1 tsp	5 ml
Large eggs	4	4
Apple juice	1/4 cup	50 ml
Apple brandy	½ cup	125 ml
Butter, melted	1 cup	250 ml
Apple, peeled and grated	1 cup	250 ml
Sweetened dried cranberries	1 cup	250 ml

Preheat oven to 325°F (160°C). Generously grease a large (12 cup) Bundt pan with shortening.

Combine flour, sugar, baking powder, and salt in a large mixing bowl. Add in eggs and apple juice, beating until smooth. Carefully add apple brandy and melted butter to the mix, mixing on medium speed until smooth. Fold in grated apple and dried cranberries, pour into prepared Bundt pan and smooth top.

Bake until golden and knife inserted into center of batter comes out clean and cake springs back - about 55 minutes. Remove from oven, cool cake in pan for 10 minutes before turning out onto serving platter.

Cupcakes

What could be more fun that mini cakes piled with frosting? Mini cakes flavored with liqueur, spirits, and/or beer and piled with frosting!

Any of these recipes can be used to bake a regular cake. Each recipe will make a 9 x 12 cake (bake for about 35 minutes), two 8" rounds (bake for about 35 minutes), or a 12" round (bake for 45-50 minutes).

Of course, in order to make a proper cupcake, you'll need frosting. Let's start you off with a couple of foundation recipes, shall we?

American Buttercream

American buttercream (also known as "country buttercream", and "decorator's buttercream") is the most common frosting. This sweet and thick frosting is a cheaper and easier alternative to real buttercream.

Butter, softened	1 cup	250 ml
Icing (powdered) sugar	2 lbs	1000 g
Milk	1/4 cup	50 ml
Flavoring (See individual recipes)		

Whip butter until smooth. Slowly add powdered sugar a bit at a time, until incorporated completely. Beat on high for 1 minute – mixture will be very, very thick.

Lower mixer speed to lowest setting, and slowly add ½ of the milk. Beat until fully incorporated and smooth. Add flavoring, beating until smooth. Once incorporated, check for consistency. Add more milk or sugar to achieve the consistency you want or need.

Swiss Meringue Buttercream

Swiss meringue buttercream is my absolute favorite frosting, and the only one I use. It is absolutely worth the bit of extra effort!

Egg whites*	5	5
Sugar (NOT powdered!)	1 cup	250 ml
Unsalted butter	1 ½ cups	375 ml
Flavoring (See individual recipes)		

Mix egg whites and sugar in a very clean metal mixing bowl, and place over a pot of simmering water on your stove top. Whisk occasionally until it hits 160°F (72°C) on a candy thermometer.

Move egg mixture to your stand mixer and whip on high (using the whisk attachment) until stiff peaks form, and mixture is relatively cool. While waiting, cut up the butter into chunks. When meringue has reached the stiff peaks stage, switch to low speed and add the butter a chunk at a time. Add flavoring, continuing to mix until fully incorporated

Once butter and flavoring are incorporated into the mix, turn speed back up to high and whip until you have a smooth buttercream. It will go through some weird stages before this point – soupy, maybe curdled. Don't worry! It will come together!

* Be VERY careful when separating your eggs. Even the slightest speck of egg yolk in the whites will prevent this frosting from properly whipping up!

Note: This frosting gets VERY hard if chilled. Always serve cakes at room temperature!

Whisky and Coke Cupcakes

Cake flour	2 cups	500 ml
Sugar	1 ½ cups	375 ml
Baking powder	4 tsp	20 ml
Salt	1 tsp	5 ml
Instant vanilla pudding mix	3 ½ oz	96 g
Large eggs	4	4
Cola of choice	½ cup	125 ml
Whisky	½ cup	125 ml
Butter, melted	½ cup	125 ml
Frosting recipe	1	1
Whisky	3 Tbsp	45 ml

Preheat oven to 350°F (180°C). Line 2 regular muffin pans with papers.

Combine flour, sugar, baking powder, salt, and pudding mix in a large mixing bowl. Add in eggs and cola, beating until smooth. Carefully add whisky and melted butter to the mix, mixing on medium speed until smooth.

Spoon into prepared muffin pans - I like to use an ice cream or cookie scoop. Bake until golden and knife inserted into center of batter comes out clean and cake springs back - about 20 minutes. Allow to cool completely before frosting

Prepare either American or Swiss meringue buttercream, following the applicable recipe, using whisky to flavor. Spoon or pipe onto cupcakes as desired. Makes about 2 dozen

Limoncello Cupcakes

Cake flour	2 cups	500 ml
Sugar	1 ½ cups	375 ml
Baking powder	4 tsp	20 ml
Salt	1 tsp	5 ml
Instant vanilla pudding mix	3 ½ oz	96 g
Large eggs	4	4
Water	½ cup	125 ml
Limoncello	½ cup	125 ml
Butter, melted	½ cup	125 ml
Zest of 2 lemons		
Frosting recipe	1	1
Limoncello	3 Tbsp	45 ml
Zest of ½ - 1 lemon		

Preheat oven to 350°F (180°C). Line 2 regular muffin pans with papers.

Combine flour, sugar, baking powder, salt, and pudding mix in a large mixing bowl. Add in eggs and water, beating until smooth. Carefully add Limoncello and melted butter to the mix, mixing on medium speed until smooth. Fold in lemon zest.

Spoon into prepared muffin pans - I like to use an ice cream or cookie scoop. Bake until golden and knife inserted into center of batter comes out clean and cake springs back - about 20 minutes. Allow to cool completely before frosting

Prepare either American or Swiss meringue buttercream, following the applicable recipe, using Limoncello and lemon zest.. Spoon or pipe onto cupcakes as desired. Makes about 2 dozen

Chocolate Chambord Cupcakes

Cake flour	2 cups	500 ml
Cocoa	1/4 cup	50 ml
Sugar	1 ½ cups	375 ml
Baking powder	4 tsp	20 ml
Salt	1 tsp	5 ml
Instant vanilla pudding mix	3 ½ oz	96 g
Large eggs	4	4
Water	½ cup	125 ml
Chambord liqueur	½ cup	125 ml
Butter, melted	½ cup	125 ml
Frosting recipe	1	1
Cocoa	1/4 cup	50 ml
Chambord	3 Tbsp	45 ml

Preheat oven to 350°F (180°C). Line 2 regular muffin pans with papers.

Combine flour, cocoa, sugar, baking powder, salt, and pudding mix in a large mixing bowl. Add in eggs and water, beating until smooth. Carefully add Chambord and melted butter to the mix, mixing on medium speed until smooth.

Spoon into prepared muffin pans - I like to use an ice cream or cookie scoop. Bake until golden and knife inserted into center of batter comes out clean and cake springs back - about 20 minutes. Allow to cool completely before frosting

Prepare either American or Swiss meringue buttercream, following the applicable recipe, using cocoa and Chambord for flavoring. Spoon or pipe onto cupcakes as desired. Makes about 2 dozen

Lynchburg Lemonade Cupcakes

Cake flour	2 cups	500 ml
Sugar	1 ½ cups	375 ml
Baking powder	4 tsp	20 ml
Salt	1 tsp	5 ml
Instant vanilla pudding mix	3 ½ oz	96 g
Large eggs	4	4
Lemon-lime soda	½ cup	125 ml
Tennessee whisky	1/4 cup	50 ml
Sweet and sour	1/4 cup	50 ml
Triple sec	2 Tbsp	30 ml
Butter, melted	½ cup	125 ml
Zest of 1 lemon		
Frosting recipe	1	1
Sweet and sour	2 Tbsp	30 ml
Tennessee whisky	1 Tbsp	15 ml
Zest of 1 lemon		

Preheat oven to 350°F (180°C). Line 2 regular muffin pans with papers.

Combine flour, sugar, baking powder, salt, and pudding mix in a large mixing bowl. Add in eggs and lemon-lime soda, beating until smooth. Carefully add whisky, sweet and sour, triple sec, and melted butter to the mix, mixing on medium speed until smooth. Fold in lemon zest.

Spoon into prepared muffin pans I like to use an ice cream or cookie scoop. Bake until golden and knife inserted into center of batter comes out clean and cake springs back - about 20 minutes. Allow to cool completely before frosting

Prepare either American or Swiss meringue buttercream, following the applicable recipe, using sweet and sour, whiskey, and lemon zest to flavor. Spoon or pipe onto cupcakes as desired.

Makes about 2 dozen

Lynchburg Lemonade Cupcakes

75

Pink Grapefruit Daiquiri Cupcakes

Cake flour	2 cups	500 ml
Sugar	1 ½ cups	375 ml
Baking powder	4 tsp	20 ml
Salt	1 tsp	5 ml
Instant vanilla pudding mix	3 ½ oz	96 g
Large eggs	4	4
Rum	½ cup	125 ml
Fresh pink grapefruit juice	½ cup	125 ml
Butter, melted	½ cup	125 ml
Zest of 1 pink grapefruit		
Red food coloring, optional		
Frosting recipe	1	1
Rum	1 Tbsp	15 ml
Pink Grapefruit Juice	2 Tbsp	30 ml
Zest of 1 Pink Grapefruit		
Red food coloring, optional		

Preheat oven to 350°F (180°C). Line 2 regular muffin pans with papers.

Combine flour, sugar, baking powder, salt, and pudding mix in a large mixing bowl. Add in eggs and Rum, beating until smooth. Carefully add pink grapefruit juice and melted butter to the mix, mixing on medium speed until smooth. Fold in grapefruit zest, add a couple drops of red food coloring if you'd like a pink colored cupcake.

Spoon into prepared muffin pans - I like to use an ice cream or cookie scoop. Bake until golden and knife inserted into center of batter comes out clean and cake springs back - about 20 minutes. Allow to cool completely before frosting

Prepare either American or Swiss meringue buttercream, following the applicable recipe, using rum, grapefruit juice, and zest to flavor. Use 1-2 drops of food coloring to color frosting pink (optional). Spoon or pipe onto cupcakes as desired.

Makes about 2 dozen

White Chocolate Almond Amaretto Cupcakes

Cake flour	2 cups	500 ml
Sugar	1 ½ cups	375 ml
Baking powder	4 tsp	20 ml
Salt	1 tsp	5 ml
Instant vanilla pudding mix	3 ½ oz	96 g
Large eggs	4	4
Almond butter, room temp	½ cup	125 ml
Water	2/3 cup	150 ml
Amaretto	1/3 cup	75 ml
Butter, melted	½ cup	125 ml
White chocolate chips, melted	1 cup	250 ml
Frosting recipe	1	1
Amaretto	3 Tbsp	45 ml
Almond butter, room temp	2 tbsp	30 ml
White chocolate chips, melted	½ cup	125 ml

Preheat oven to 350°F (180°C). Line 2 regular muffin pans with papers.

Combine flour, sugar, baking powder, salt, and pudding mix in a large mixing bowl. Add in eggs and almond butter, beating until smooth. Carefully add water, amaretto, and melted butter to the mix, mixing on medium speed until smooth. Carefully pour melted white chocolate chips into batter, continuing to mix until well incorporated.

Spoon into prepared muffin pans - I like to use an ice cream or cookie scoop. Bake until golden and knife inserted into center of batter comes out clean and cake springs back - about 20 minutes. Allow to cool completely before frosting

Prepare either American or Swiss meringue buttercream, following the applicable recipe, using amaretto, almond butter, and melted white chocolate chips to flavor. Spoon or pipe onto cupcakes as desired.

Makes about 2 dozen

Guinness Chocolate Cupcakes

Cake flour	2 cups	500 ml
Cocoa	3/4 cup	175 ml
Sugar	2 cups	500 ml
Baking powder	4 tsp	20 ml
Salt	1 tsp	5 ml
Sour cream	½ cup	125 ml
Large eggs	4	4
Butter, melted	½ cup	125 ml
Guinness (or other stout beer)	1 cup	250 ml
Frosting recipe	1	1
Cream cheese, softened	½ cup	125 ml
Guinness (or other stout beer)	3 Tbsp	45 ml

Preheat oven to 350°F (180°C). Line 2 regular muffin pans with papers.

Combine flour, cocoa, sugar, baking powder, and salt in a large mixing bowl. Add in sour cream, eggs and melted butter, beating until smooth. Carefully add Guinness to the mix, mixing on medium speed until smooth.

Spoon into prepared muffin pans - I like to use an ice cream or cookie scoop. Bake until knife inserted into center of batter comes out clean and cake springs back - about 20 minutes. Allow to cool completely before frosting

Prepare either American or Swiss meringue buttercream, following the applicable recipe, using softened cream cheese and Guinness for flavoring. Spoon or pipe onto cupcakes as desired. Makes about 2 dozen

French Martini Cupcakes

Cake flour	2 cups	500 ml
Sugar	1 ½ cups	375 ml
Baking powder	4 tsp	20 ml
Salt	1 tsp	5 ml
Instant vanilla pudding mix	3 ½ oz	96 g
Large eggs	4	4
Chambord	1/3 cup	75 ml
Pineapple juice	2/3 cup	150 ml
Butter, melted	½ cup	125 ml
Crushed pineapple	1 cup	250 ml
Frosting recipe	1	1
Chambord	3 Tbsp	45 ml

Preheat oven to 350°F (180°C). Line 2 regular muffin pans with papers.

Combine flour, sugar, baking powder, salt, and pudding mix in a large mixing bowl. Add in eggs and Chambord, beating until smooth. Carefully add pineapple juice and melted butter to the mix, mixing on medium speed until smooth. Fold in crushed pineapple.

Spoon into prepared muffin pans - I like to use an ice cream or cookie scoop. Bake until golden and knife inserted into center of batter comes out clean and cake springs back - about 20 minutes. Allow to cool completely before frosting

Prepare either American or Swiss meringue buttercream, following the applicable recipe, using Chambord to flavor. Spoon or pipe onto cupcakes as desired. Makes about 2 dozen

Mimosa Cupcakes

Cake flour	2 cups	500 ml
Sugar	1 ½ cups	375 ml
Baking powder	4 tsp	20 ml
Salt	1 tsp	5 ml
Instant vanilla pudding mix	3 ½ oz	96 g
Large eggs	4	4
Orange juice	½ cup	125 ml
Champagne	½ cup	125 ml
Butter, melted	½ cup	125 ml
Zest of 1 orange		
Frosting recipe	1	1
Champagne	3 Tbsp	45 ml
Zest of 1 orange		

Preheat oven to 350°F (180°C). Line 2 regular muffin pans with papers.

Combine flour, sugar, baking powder, salt, and pudding mix in a large mixing bowl. Add in eggs and orange juice, beating until smooth. Carefully add champagne and melted butter to the mix, mixing on medium speed until smooth. Fold in orange zest.

Spoon into prepared muffin pans - I like to use an ice cream or cookie scoop. Bake until golden and knife inserted into center of batter comes out clean and cake springs back - about 20 minutes. Allow to cool completely before frosting

Prepare either American or Swiss meringue buttercream, following the applicable recipe, using champagne and orange zest for flavoring. Spoon or pipe onto cupcakes as desired.

Makes about 2 dozen

Bellini Cupcakes

Cake flour	2 cups	500 ml
Sugar	1 ½ cups	375 ml
Baking powder	4 tsp	20 ml
Salt	1 tsp	5 ml
Instant vanilla pudding mix	3 ½ oz	96 g
Large eggs	4	4
Butter, melted	½ cup	125 ml
Champagne	1 cup	250 ml
Large peaches, peeled and grated	2	2
Frosting recipe	1	1
Champagne	3 Tbsp	45 ml
1 Peach, thinly sliced		

Preheat oven to 350°F (180°C). Line 2 regular muffin pans with papers.

Combine flour, sugar, baking powder, salt, and pudding mix in a large mixing bowl. Add in eggs, beating until smooth. Carefully add melted butter and champagne to the mix, mixing on medium speed until smooth.

Fold grated peaches into cupcake batter, then spoon into prepared muffin pans - I like to use an ice cream or cookie scoop. Bake until golden and knife inserted into center of batter comes out clean and cake springs back - about 20 minutes. Allow to cool completely before frosting

Prepare either American or Swiss meringue buttercream, following the applicable recipe, using Champagne to flavor Spoon or pipe onto cupcakes as desired, garnish with peach slices.

Makes about 2 dozen

Sex on the Beach Torte

Sweetened dried cranberries	2/3 cup	150 ml
Peach schnapps	1/3 cup	75 ml
Cake flour	3 cups	750 ml
Sugar	2 1/4 cups	550 ml
Baking powder	2 Tbsp	30 ml
Salt	1 ½ tsp	7 ml
Instant vanilla pudding mix	3 ½ oz	96 g
Eggs	6	6
Peach schnapps	½ cup	125 ml
Orange juice	1 cup	250 ml
Butter, melted	1 ½ cups	375 ml
Zest of 1 orange		
Frosting recipe	1	1
Zest of ½ an orange		

Mix together sweetened dried cranberries and peach schnapps. Allow to marinate overnight.

Preheat oven to 350°F (180°C). Liberally grease two 8" or 10" round cake pans with vegetable shortening, and/or spray with baking spray.

Combine flour, sugar, baking powder, salt, and pudding mix in a large mixing bowl. Add in eggs and peach schnapps, beating until smooth. Carefully add orange juice and melted butter to the mix, mixing on medium speed until smooth. Fold in orange zest.

Divide batter among prepared cake pans. Bake until golden and knife inserted into center of batter comes out clean and cake springs back - about 45-60 minutes. Allow to cool 10-15 minutes before turning cakes out onto baking rack to cool fully. Ideally, allow to cool to room temperature, wrap tightly with plastic wrap, and proceed with the following steps the next day.

Prepare either American or Swiss meringue buttercream, following the applicable recipe. Process marinated cranberries - along with any peach schnapps that hasn't absorbed - in a blender or food processor until cranberries are finely chopped. Mix in to prepared buttercream, along with orange zest.

Remove plastic wrap from cake layers. Carefully slice the top off each round, leveling the surface of the cake. Place one cake, cut side up, on cake plate. Fill with buttercream, and top off with second cake round, cut side down. Frost sides and top of cake

Bahama Mama Torte

Bahama Mama Torte

Cake flour	3 cups	750 ml
Sugar	2 1/4 cups	550 ml
Baking powder	2 Tbsp	30 ml
Salt	1 ½ tsp	7 ml
Instant vanilla pudding mix	3 ½ oz	96 g
Eggs	6	6
White rum	½ cup	125 ml
Pineapple juice	1 ½ cup	375 ml
Butter, melted	1 ½ cups	375 ml
Frosting recipe	1	1
Kahlua	2 Tbsp	30 ml
Malibu rum	2 Tbsp	30 ml
Kahlua	1/4 cup	50 ml
Malibu rum	1/4 cup	50 ml

Preheat oven to 350°F (180°C). Liberally grease two 8" or 10" round cake pans with vegetable shortening, and/or spray with baking spray.

Combine flour, sugar, baking powder, salt, and pudding mix in a large mixing bowl. Add in eggs and white rum, beating until smooth. Carefully add pineapple juice and melted butter to the mix, mixing on medium speed until smooth.

Divide batter among prepared cake pans. Bake until golden and knife inserted into center of batter comes out clean and cake springs back - about 45-60 minutes. Allow to cool 10-15 minutes before turning cakes out onto baking rack to cool fully. Ideally, allow to cool to room temperature, wrap tightly with plastic wrap, and proceed with the following steps the next day.

Prepare either American or Swiss meringue buttercream, following the applicable recipe, using 2 Tbsp (30 ml) each of Malibu rum and Kahlua to flavor.

Remove plastic wrap from cake layers. Carefully slice the top off each round, leveling the surface of the cake. Mix together 1/4 cup (50 ml) each of Malibu rum and Kahlua, brush cut surfaces of cakes liberally with the mixture.

Place one cake, cut side up, on cake plate. Fill with prepared buttercream, and top off with second cake round, cut side down. Frost sides and top of cake.

B-52 Torte

B-52 Torte

Cake flour	3 cups	750 ml
Sugar	2 1/4 cups	550 ml
Baking powder	2 Tbsp	30 ml
Salt	1 ½ tsp	7 ml
Instant vanilla pudding mix	3 ½ oz	96 g
Eggs	6	6
Water	1 cup	250 ml
Butter, melted	1 ½ cups	375 ml
Coffee	1/4 cup	50 ml
Cocoa	3 Tbsp	45 ml
Grand Marnier	1/4 cup	50 ml
Orange food coloring, optional		
Heavy cream	1/2 cup	150 ml
Grand Marnier	2 tbsp	30 ml
Butter	2 Tbsp	30 ml
Milk chocolate chips	2 cups	500 ml
Frosting recipe	1	1
Cocoa	3 Tbsp	45 ml
Bailey's Irish cream	3 Tbsp	45 ml

Preheat oven to 350°F (180°C). Liberally grease two 8" or 10" round cake pans with vegetable shortening, and/or spray with baking spray.

Combine flour, sugar, baking powder, salt, and pudding mix in a large mixing bowl. Add in eggs, beating until smooth. Carefully add water and melted butter to the mix, mixing on medium speed until smooth.   Divide batter equally into 2 bowls. In one bowl, add cocoa powder and coffee to the batter, stirring until well incorporated and smooth. In the second bowl, add Grand Marnier and 2-3 drops of orange food coloring, if desired. Stir until well incorporated and smooth.

Pour batter into prepared cake pans, one flavor per pan. Bake until golden and knife inserted into center of batter comes out clean and cake springs back - about 45-60 minutes. Allow to cool 10-15 minutes before turning cakes out onto baking rack to cool fully. Ideally, allow to cool to room temperature, wrap tightly with plastic wrap, and proceed with the following steps the next day.

In a small saucepan, combine heavy cream, Grand Marnier, and butter. Heat until butter is melted, bring to a simmer. In a glass bowl, pour cream mixture over chocolate chips, allow to sit for 5 minutes. Gently stir until chocolate is completely melted, cream has fully incorporated, and everything is smooth. Allow to cool to room temperature. Once cool, beat with a wooden spoon until smooth but thick. This is chocolate ganache.

Prepare either American or Swiss meringue buttercream, following the applicable recipe, using cocoa and Irish cream to flavor.

Remove plastic wrap from cake layers. Carefully slice the top off each round, leveling the surface of the cake. Carefully cut each cake in half, height-wise, for 4 thin rounds of cake in all.

Place one round of Grand Marnier cake on cake plate, spread with a thick layer of chocolate ganache. Top with one round of mocha cake, spread with a thick layer of Irish cream buttercream. Top with another round of Grand Marnier cake. Spread with a final thick layer of chocolate ganache, and top with remaining layer of mocha cake.

Chill for 30 minutes before frosting sides and top of cake with remaining buttercream. Serve at room temperature.

Tiramisu Torte

Cake flour	3 cups	750 ml
Sugar	2 1/4 cups	550 ml
Baking powder	2 Tbsp	30 ml
Salt	1 ½ tsp	7 ml
Instant vanilla pudding mix	3 ½ oz	96 g
Eggs	6	6
Amaretto	3/4 cup	175 ml
Water	3/4 cup	175 ml
Butter, melted	1 ½ cups	375 ml
Heavy cream	2/3 cup	150 ml
Kahlua	2 tbsp	30 ml
Butter	2 Tbsp	30 ml
Dark chocolate chips	2 cups	500 ml
Swiss meringue buttercream recipe	1	1
Mascarpone cheese, softened	1 cup	50 ml
Amaretto	3 tbsp	45 ml
Kahlua	1/3 cup	75 ml

Preheat oven to 350°F (180°C). Liberally grease two 8" or 10" round cake pans with vegetable shortening, and/or spray with baking spray.

Combine flour, sugar, baking powder, salt, and pudding mix in a large mixing bowl. Add in eggs and amaretto, beating until smooth. Carefully add water and melted butter to the mix, mixing on medium speed until smooth.

Divide batter among prepared cake pans. Bake until golden and knife inserted into center of batter comes out clean and cake springs back - about 45-60 minutes. Allow to cool 10-15 minutes before turning cakes out onto baking rack to cool fully. Ideally, allow to cool to room temperature, wrap tightly with plastic wrap, and proceed with the following steps the next day.

In a small saucepan, combine heavy cream, Kahlua, and butter. Heat until butter is melted, bring to a simmer. In a glass bowl, pour cream mixture over chocolate chips, allow to sit for 5 minutes. Gently stir until chocolate is completely melted, cream has fully incorporated, and everything is smooth. Allow to cool to room temperature. This is chocolate ganache.

Prepare Swiss Meringue buttercream, following the applicable recipe, beating in softened mascarpone cheese and amaretto to flavor.

Remove plastic wrap from cake layers. Carefully slice the top off each round, leveling the surface of the cake. Carefully cut each cake in half, horizontally, for 4 thin rounds of cake in all. Brush cut surfaces of cakes liberally with the 1/3 cup (75 ml) Kahlua.

Place one round, cut side up, on cake plate. Spread with chocolate ganache, then a layer of mascarpone buttercream. Top off with second cake round, spread with chocolate ganache, then a layer of mascarpone buttercream. Repeat a third time, top off with final round of cake. Chill for 30 minutes before frosting sides and top of cake with remaining buttercream. Serve at room temperature.

"Southern Belle" Torte

Cake flour	3 cups	750 ml
Sugar	2 1/4 cups	550 ml
Baking powder	2 Tbsp	30 ml
Salt	1 ½ tsp	7 ml
Instant vanilla pudding mix	3 ½ oz	96 g
Eggs	6	6
Water	3/4 cup	175 ml
Amaretto	3/4 cup	175 ml
Butter, melted	1 ½ cups	375 ml
Peach syrup*	1/4 cup	50 ml
Southern Comfort	1/4 cup	50 ml
Sugar	1/4 cup	50 ml
Frosting recipe	1	1
Southern Comfort	3 Tbsp	45 ml

1 large can of peaches, drained and thinly sliced

Preheat oven to 350°F (180°C). Liberally grease two 8" or 10" round cake pans with vegetable shortening, and/or spray with baking spray.

Combine flour, sugar, baking powder, salt, and pudding mix in a large mixing bowl. Add in eggs and water, beating until smooth. Carefully add amaretto and melted butter to the mix, mixing on medium speed until smooth.

Divide batter among prepared cake pans. Bake until golden and knife inserted into center of batter comes out clean and cake springs back - about 45-60 minutes. Allow to cool 10-15 minutes before turning cakes out onto baking rack to cool fully. Ideally, allow to cool to room temperature, wrap tightly with plastic wrap, and proceed with the following steps the next day.

In a small saucepan, combine peach syrup (* reserved from canned peaches), Southern Comfort, and sugar. Heat to a simmer, stirring until sugar is dissolved. Remove from heat, cool to room temperature.

Prepare either American or Swiss Meringue buttercream, following the applicable recipe, using 3 Tbsp (45 ml) Southern Comfort to flavor.

Remove plastic wrap from cake layers. Carefully slice the top off each round, leveling the surface of the cake. Brush cut surfaces of cakes liberally with the peach juice / Southern Comfort mixture.

Place one cake, cut side up, on cake plate. Spread with a moderate layer of Southern Comfort buttercream, and arrange peach slices on top, allowing frosting to poke up between slices. Top off with second cake round, cut side down. Cover with plastic wrap, chill for 30 minutes before frosting sides and top of cake.

Bread Puddings

Bread pudding is an easy and comforting dessert, especially great on cold winter days. Here are a few favorites!

Basic Bread Pudding with Boozy Sauce

1 Loaf of day old French or Italian bread

Butter, melted	1/4 cup	50 ml
Milk	3 cups	750 ml
Eggs, beaten	6	6
Sugar	1 ½ cups	375 ml
Raisins or nuts (optional)	1 cup	250 ml
Butter, melted	½ cup	125 ml
Sugar	1 cup	250 ml
Egg	1	1
Whisky or brandy	½ cup	125 ml

Preheat oven to 350°F (180°C). Lightly grease 9" x 12" square baking pan with vegetable shortening or butter.

Rip bread into bite sized pieces (about 6 cups worth). Cover with melted butter and milk, stirring to coat the bread pieces. Allow all of the milk to soak in, then arrange into prepared baking pan.

Combine beaten eggs and sugar in a mixing bowl. Whisk until fully combined and smooth. Pour over bread, stirring lightly so that all of the bread is covered. Gently stir in nuts and/or raisins, if using.

Bake in the preheated oven for 45 minutes, or until set. Edges should be golden, and easily pull away from the side of the pan.

Combine melted butter, sugar, and egg in a small saucepan, whisking until well blended. Whisk constantly, cooking over low heat until mixture thickens - do not allow mixture to come to a simmer. Whisk in whisky or brandy, remove from heat - sauce should be smooth and creamy.
Serve bread pudding hot, with sauce poured over each serving. Best eaten the same day it is made. 8-10 servings.

Basic Boozy Bread Pudding

1 Loaf of day old French or Italian bread		
Butter, melted	1/4 cup	50 ml
Milk	2 cups	500 ml
Eggs, beaten	6	6
Liqueur of choice*	1 cup	250 ml
Sugar	1 ½ cups	375 ml
Fruit/nuts (optional)	1 cup	250 ml

Preheat oven to 350°F (180°C). Lightly grease 9" x 12" square baking pan with vegetable shortening or butter.

Rip bread into bite sized pieces (about 6 cups worth). Cover with melted butter and milk, stirring to coat the bread pieces. Allow all of the milk to soak in, then arrange into prepared baking pan.

Combine beaten eggs, liqueur, and sugar in a mixing bowl. Whisk until fully combined and smooth. Pour over bread, stirring lightly so that all of the bread is covered. Gently stir in nuts and/or raisins, if using.

Bake in the preheated oven for 45 minutes, or until set. Edges should be golden, and easily pull away from the side of the pan. Serve hot, preferably the same day it is made. 8-10 servings.

*Almost liqueur can be used. If using a cream base liqueur, follow the recipe as is. For a non cream based liqueur, substitute 1 cup (250 ml) heavy cream for 1 cup of the milk.

Basic Chocolate Boozy Bread Pudding

1 Loaf of day old French or Italian bread		
Butter, melted	1/4 cup	50 ml
Heavy cream	1 cup	250 ml
Chocolate chips	1 cup	250 ml
Milk	1 cup	250 ml
Eggs, beaten	6	6
Cocoa	1/3 cup	75 ml
Liqueur of choice	1 cup	250 ml
Sugar	1 1/4 cups	300 ml
Dried fruit or nuts (optional)	1 cup	250 ml

Lightly grease 9" x 12" square baking pan with vegetable shortening or butter. Rip bread into bite sized pieces (about 6 cups worth), toss with melted butter. Arrange in prepared baking pan.

In a small saucepan, heat heavy cream to a simmer. In a glass bowl, pour cream mixture over chocolate chips, allow to sit for 5 minutes. Gently stir until chocolate is completely melted, cream has fully incorporated, and everything is smooth.

Combine milk, eggs, cocoa, liqueur, and sugar in a medium saucepan. Whisk until well combined and smooth. Whisk constantly over low heat until just warm, combine with still-warm white chocolate mix. Pour over bread, stirring lightly so that all of the bread is covered. Gently stir in fruit or nuts, if using. Allow to rest for 1 hour.

Preheat oven to 350°F (180°C).

Bake for 45 minutes, or until set. Edges should be golden, and easily pull away from the side of the pan. Serve hot, preferably the same day it is made. 8-10 servings.

Flavor ideas:

Mudslide: Use milk chocolate chips, and ½ cup (50 ml) each Bailey's Irish Cream and Kahlua for liqueur. Great with sliced almonds!

Jagermeister: Use dark chocolate chips, 2/3 cup (150 ml) of Jagermiester for liqueur. Increase milk by 1/3 cup (75 ml), increase sugar by 1/4 cup (50 ml)

Dark Chocolate Raspberry: Use dark chocolate, Chambord for liqueur. Dried raspberries soaked in 1/4 cup (50 ml) Chambord overnight really completes it.

Tropical Melon: Use white chocolate chips, ½ cup (125 ml) each of creme de banane and melon liqueur. Add in 1 cup coconut for the fruit/nuts

White Chocolate Amaretto Bread Pudding

1 Loaf of day old French or Italian bread		
Butter, melted	1/4 cup	50 ml
Heavy cream	1 cup	250 ml
White chocolate chips	1 cup	250 ml
Milk	1 cup	250 ml
Eggs, beaten	6	6
Amaretto	1 cup	250 ml
Sugar	1 1/4 cups	300 ml
Sliced almonds (optional)	1 cup	250 ml
White Chocolate Amaretto sauce (optional, recipe follows)		

Lightly grease 9" x 12" square baking pan with vegetable shortening or butter. Rip bread into bite sized pieces (about 6 cups worth), toss with melted butter. Arrange in prepared baking pan.

In a small saucepan, heat heavy cream to a simmer. In a glass bowl, pour cream mixture over chocolate chips, allow to sit for 5 minutes. Gently stir until chocolate is completely melted, cream has fully incorporated, and everything is smooth.

Combine milk, eggs, amaretto and sugar in a medium saucepan. Whisk until well combined and smooth. Whisk constantly over low heat until just warm, combine with still-warm white chocolate mix. Pour over bread, stirring lightly so that all of the bread is covered. Gently stir in almonds, if using. Allow to rest for 1 hour.

Preheat oven to 350°F (180°C). Once heated, bake for 45 minutes, or until set. Edges should be golden, and easily pull away from the side of the pan. Serve hot, preferably the same day it is made. 8-10 servings.

White Chocolate Amaretto Sauce

White Chocolate Amaretto Bread Pudding is quite rich on its own, but this sauce can be served over it. The addition of this sauce really sends it over the top!

Heavy cream	½ cup	125 ml
Amaretto	3 Tbsp	45 ml
Butter	2 Tbsp	30 ml
White chocolate chips	1 cup	250 ml

In a small saucepan, heat heavy cream, amaretto, and butter to a simmer. In a glass bowl, pour cream mixture over white chocolate chips, allow to sit for 5 minutes. Gently stir until chocolate is completely melted, cream has fully incorporated, and everything is smooth. Serve warm.

Rum Raisin Bread Pudding

Raisins	2 cups	500 ml
Amber rum	1 cup	250 ml
1 Loaf of day old French or Italian bread		
Butter, melted	1/4 cup	50 ml
Milk	2 cups	500 ml
Amber rum	1 cup	250 ml
Eggs, beaten	6	6
Sugar	1 ½ cups	375 ml
Butter, melted	½ cup	125 ml
Sugar	1 cup	250 ml
Egg	1	1
Amber rum	½ cup	125 ml

The day before making bread pudding, cover raisins with rum. Allow to soak overnight.

Preheat oven to 350°F (180°C). Lightly grease 9" x 12" square baking pan with vegetable shortening or butter.

Rip bread into bite sized pieces (about 6 cups worth). Cover with melted butter and milk, stirring to coat the bread pieces. Allow all of the milk to soak in, then arrange into prepared baking pan.

Combine rum, beaten eggs and sugar in a mixing bowl. Whisk until fully combined and smooth. Pour over bread, stirring lightly so that all of the bread is covered. Gently stir in raisins. Bake in the preheated oven for 45 minutes, or until set. Edges should be golden, and easily pull away from the side of the pan.

Combine melted butter, sugar, and egg in a small saucepan, whisking until well blended. Whisk constantly, cooking over low heat until mixture thickens - do not allow mixture to come to a simmer. Whisk in rum, remove from heat - sauce should be smooth and creamy.

Serve bread pudding hot, with sauce poured over each serving. Best eaten the same day it is made.

8-10 servings.

Raspberry-Peach Bread Pudding

1 Loaf of day old French or Italian bread		
Butter, melted	1/4 cup	50 ml
Milk	2 1/3 cups	575 ml
Peach schnapps	2/3 cup	150 ml
Eggs, beaten	6	6
Sugar	1 ½ cups	375 ml
Fresh peaches, sliced	2-3	2-3
Fresh raspberries	1 cup	250 ml
Butter, melted	½ cup	125 ml
Sugar	1 cup	250 ml
Egg	1	1
Chambord	2/3 cup	150 ml

Preheat oven to 350°F (180°C). Lightly grease 9" x 12" square baking pan with vegetable shortening or butter.

Rip bread into bite sized pieces (about 6 cups worth). Cover with melted butter and milk, stirring to coat the bread pieces. Allow all of the milk to soak in, then arrange into prepared baking pan.

Combine peach schnapps, beaten eggs and sugar in a mixing bowl. Whisk until fully combined and smooth. Pour over bread, stirring lightly so that all of the bread is covered. Gently stir in peach slices and raspberries. Bake in the preheated oven for 45 minutes, or until set. Edges should be golden, and easily pull away from the side of the pan.

Combine melted butter, sugar, and egg in a small saucepan, whisking until well blended. Whisk constantly, cooking over low heat until mixture thickens - do not allow mixture to come to a simmer. Whisk in Chambord, remove from heat - sauce should be smooth and creamy.

Serve bread pudding hot, with sauce poured over each serving. Best eaten the same day it is made.

8-10 servings.

Raspberry-Peach Bread Pudding

Black Walnut Bread Pudding

1 Loaf of day old French or Italian bread		
Butter, melted	1/4 cup	50 ml
Milk	2 1/2 cups	625 ml
Eggs, beaten	6	6
Black walnut liqueur	½ cup	125 ml
Sugar	1 ½ cups	375 ml
Black Walnuts, chopped	1 ½ cups	375 ml

Preheat oven to 350°F (180°C). Lightly grease 9" x 12" square baking pan with vegetable shortening or butter.

Rip bread into bite sized pieces (about 6 cups worth). Cover with melted butter and milk, stirring to coat the bread pieces. Allow all of the milk to soak in, then arrange into prepared baking pan.

Combine beaten eggs, liqueur, and sugar in a mixing bowl. Whisk until fully combined and smooth. Pour over bread, stirring lightly so that all of the bread is covered. Gently stir in walnuts

Bake in the preheated oven for 45 minutes, or until set. Edges should be golden, and easily pull away from the side of the pan. Serve hot, preferably the same day it is made. 8-10 servings.

Pina Colada Bread Pudding

1 Loaf of day old French or Italian bread		
Butter, melted	1/4 cup	50 ml
Pina colada mix	1 ½ cups	375 ml
Milk	½ cup	125 ml
Amber rum	1 cup	250 ml
Eggs, beaten	6	6
Sugar	1 ½ cups	375 ml
Coconut	1 cup	250 ml
Crushed pineapple, drained	1 cup	250 ml
Butter, melted	½ cup	125 ml
Sugar	1 cup	250 ml
Egg	1	1
Amber rum	½ cup	125 ml

Preheat oven to 350°F (180°C). Lightly grease 9" x 12" square baking pan with vegetable shortening or butter.

Rip bread into bite sized pieces (about 6 cups worth). Cover with melted butter, pina colada mix and milk, stirring to coat the bread pieces. Allow all of the liquid to soak in, then arrange into prepared baking pan.

Combine rum, beaten eggs and sugar in a mixing bowl. Whisk until fully combined and smooth. Pour over bread, stirring lightly so that all of the bread is covered. Gently stir in coconut and pineapple. Bake in the preheated oven for 45 minutes, or until set. Edges should be golden, and easily pull away from the side of the pan.

Combine melted butter, sugar, and egg in a small saucepan, whisking until well blended. Whisk constantly, cooking over low heat until mixture thickens - do not allow mixture to come to a simmer. Whisk in rum, remove from heat - sauce should be smooth and creamy.

Serve bread pudding hot, with sauce poured over each serving. Best eaten the same day it is made. 8-10 servings.

Upside Down Cakes

Upside down cakes are incredibly easy to make, and pretty enough to not require any cake decorating skills!

Basic Boozy Upside Down Cake

Butter, melted	1/3 cup	75 ml
Flour	1 ½ tsp	7 ml
Brown sugar	½ cup	125 ml
Liqueur of choice	3 Tbsp	45 ml
Fruit of choice, sliced	2 cups	500 ml
Cake flour	2 cups	500 ml
Sugar	1 ½ cups	375 ml
Baking powder	4 tsp	20 ml
Salt	1 tsp	5 ml
Instant vanilla pudding mix	3 ½ oz	96 g
Large eggs	4	4
Water	½ cup	125 ml
Liqueur of choice	½ cup	125 ml
Butter, melted	3/4 cup	175 ml

Preheat oven to 325°F (160°C). Liberally grease a 10" round pan with vegetable shortening. Cut out a 10" round of parchment paper, using bottom of pan as a template. Place inside pan, smoothing it out to cling securely to the shortening.

Combine melted butter, flour, brown sugar, and liqueur in a small saucepan. Heat on low, stirring until well combined. Pour into prepared cake pan, spreading evenly. Arrange fruit slices on top of this mixture, set aside.

Combine flour, sugar, baking powder, salt, and pudding mix in a large mixing bowl. Add in eggs and water, beating until smooth. Carefully add liqueur and melted butter to the mix, mixing on medium speed until smooth. Gently pour into prepared pan. Bake until golden and knife inserted into center of batter comes out clean and cake springs back - about 50-60 minutes.

With the hot cake still in the pan, carefully level the top by cutting off the "dome" over the edge of the pan. Allow cake to cool for about 20 minutes before turning cake out directly onto serving plate.

Brandied Apple Upside Down Cake: Use apple brandy for the liqueur in both steps that call for it, and sliced apple for the fruit. Add 1/4 tsp cinnamon to brown sugar mix, and ½ tsp cinnamon to cake batter dry ingredients.

Southern Peach Upside Down Cake: Use amaretto for liqueur in first step, and sliced peaches for the fruit. (Optional: Add a handful of thinly sliced almonds or chopped pecans with the peach slices!). Use Southern Comfort for liqueur in cake batter.

Bananas Foster Upside Down Cake: Use 2 Tbsp (30 ml) rum and 1 Tbsp (15 ml) creme de banane for liqueur in first step, adding ½ tsp cinnamon. Use banana slices for fruit. For cake batter, use ½ cup (125 ml) brown sugar in place of ½ cup (125 ml) of the sugar, and add 1 tsp cinnamon to dry ingredients. Use amber rum for liqueur in batter.

Bananas Foster Upside Down Cake

Mango Mojito Upside Down Cake

This recipe may look daunting at first glance, but it really is easier than it appears. It's also my absolute favorite recipe in this book, and possibly the best cake ever created. Not kidding.

Butter, melted	1/3 cup	75 ml
Flour	1 ½ tsp	7 ml
Brown sugar	½ cup	125 ml
Amber rum	3 Tbsp	45 ml
2 cans mango slices in syrup, drained and thinly sliced		
Cake flour	2 cups	500 ml
Sugar	1 ½ cups	375 ml
Baking powder	4 tsp	20 ml
Salt	1 tsp	5 ml
Instant vanilla pudding mix	3 ½ oz	96 g
Large eggs	4	4
Amber rum	1/3 cup	75 ml
Mango pulp*	2/3 cup	150 ml
Butter, melted	½ cup	125 ml

* Mango pulp can be found in the international section of many grocery stores, or in Indian grocery stores.

Butter	1/4 cup	50 ml
Water	2 Tbsp	30 ml
Fresh mint leaves, crushed	½ cup	125 ml
Sugar	½ cup	125 ml
Amber rum	1/4 cup	50 ml

Amber rum	1/4 cup	50 ml
Fresh mint leaves, crushed	½ cup	125 ml
Powdered (Icing) Sugar	2+ cups	500+ ml

Preheat oven to 325°F (160°C). Liberally grease a 10" round pan with vegetable shortening. Cut out a 10" round of parchment paper, using bottom of pan as a template. Place inside pan, smoothing it out to cling securely to the shortening. Combine melted butter, flour, brown sugar, and rum in a small saucepan. Heat on low, stirring until well combined. Pour into prepared cake pan, spreading evenly. Arrange mango slices on top of this mixture, set aside.

Combine flour, sugar, baking powder, salt, and pudding mix in a large mixing bowl. Add in eggs and rum beating until smooth. Carefully add mango pulp and melted butter to the mix, mixing on medium speed until smooth. Carefully pour into prepared pan. Bake until golden and knife inserted into center of batter comes out clean and cake springs back - about 50-60 minutes. While cake is baking, combine butter, water, mint leaves, sugar, and rum in a small saucepan. Allow to heat to a simmer, then remove from heat and allow to cool. Once cool, strain - pressing trapped liquid out of the mint. Discard mint leaves, set syrup aside.

With the hot cake still in the pan, carefully level the top by cutting off the "dome" over the edge of the pan. Evenly pour the mint syrup over the entire cake. Allow cake to cool for about 20 minutes before turning cake out directly onto serving plate. This cake is delicate, and should not be moved to a different plate after being turned out!

While cake is cooling on serving plate, Heat 1/4 cup amber rum. Add mint leaves, and let steep for 10 minutes. Strain, once again pressing trapped liquid out of the mint. Discard mint leaves. Mix as much icing sugar into the 1/4 cup rum as it takes to make a very thick paste. Melt it in the microwave for a few seconds, then drizzle over the cake.

Gluten Free Fruitcake

Forget everything you've heard about fruitcake, and about gluten free baking. This is a gorgeous, extremely tasty fruitcake that will be loved by all – fans of regular fruitcake, fruitcake haters, people with gluten allergies, and even those who aren't restricted to gluten free. This cake has a wonderful texture – you'd never know it was gluten free. Trust me – I'm the BIGGEST snob about gluten free baked goods!

This cake, though? I'd eat this for breakfast, in addition to as a snack, or dessert. I make variations of this throughout the year, to satisfy any urge for baked goods. This is WAY too good to be designated JUST a holiday thing!

We used a mix of raisins, cranberries, cherries, apricots, and pineapple, but you can use a combination of whatever dried fruit you love. It is boozed up with Southern Comfort, which works SO well with the fruit flavors, in my opinion.

Mixed dried fruits *	2 3/4 cups	675 ml
Southern Comfort **	2/3 cups	150 ml
Butter	½ cup	125 ml
Sugar	3/4 cup	175 ml
Large eggs, separated	3	3
Vanilla extract	1 tsp	5 ml
Finely grated zest of 1 lemon		
Finely grated zest of 1 orange		
Gluten-free all purpose flour blend	1 cup	250 ml
Baking powder	1 ½ tsp	7 ml
Salt	½ tsp	2 ml
Milk	½ cup	125 ml
Chopped pecans	1 cup	500 ml

A day or two before baking the fruitcake, chop dried fruits into pieces, mix in Southern Comfort, and cover.

When ready to make the fruitcake, Preheat oven to 325F. Spray an 8" round cake pan (spring form pan works, also), and then line it with parchment paper. I like to cut a round just slightly bigger than the bottom diameter of the pan, centering it, and smoothing the edges slightly up the side of the pan, folding and easing as necessary. Then, I cut a "collar" of parchment, about 5" x 28". Fold that in half along the length, and then place that – folded side down – around the inside edge of the cake pan.

Strain dried fruit mixture, leaving it in your sieve to drain while you prepare the rest of the cookie batter. Be sure to reserve the Southern Comfort / fruit syrup that strains out!

Cream butter and sugar until light and fluffy. Add egg YOLKS (reserving the whites separately), vanilla, and zests, continue beating until eggs are fully incorporated and mixture is once again smooth and fluffy.
In a separate bowl, combine flour, baking powder, and salt. Add dry ingredients to the butter & sugar mixture, beat gently until well combined. Add milk, continuing to beat

until well combined. Add in the strained fruits, mixing once more until well combined. Set aside.

In a – very clean – mixing bowl or stand mixer, whip the egg whites on high speed, until stiff peaks form. Gently fold whipped egg whites into the main batter, until all of the "white" disappears. Gently mix in the pecans, just until well distributed.

Pour cake batter into prepared cake pan, smooth around the pan to push the parchment paper "collar" against the sides of the pan. Gently bang the pan onto a flat surface a few times to knock out any air bubbles.

Bake for about an hour and a half – hour and 45 minutes, until a knife poked into the center of the cake comes out clean.

While cake is still hot, pour reserved Southern Comfort runoff evening over the top of the cake. Allow to cool fully before removing from pan.

** If you're not a fan of Southern Comfort, use Jack Daniels, Rum, or Brandy.

Gluten Free Fruitcake

Truffles

Fancy

I know that the idea of making "fancy" desserts can seem intimidating to some. Many foo-foo desserts don't seem to come across as something that can be made at home, or at least definitely not by a beginner.

I swear that's not true of anything in this chapter! Truffles, cream puffs, baklava... all deceptively easy to make. Go ahead, try it!

Truffles

Truffles consist of two main parts - the center (chocolate ganache), and the coating. The ganache center is made from just a few very basic ingredients - chocolate, cream, flavoring, and butter. The coating can be made from almost anything - your creativity is pretty much your only limit!

Typically, you'll see store-bought truffles enrobed in chocolate. While that's certainly a popular option, it does veer off into "intimidating" territory - tempering chocolate, etc. Personally, I don't bother - I find rolling truffles in various non-chocolate coatings is not only more fun and less work, I prefer the taste. Tempering chocolate (required for chocolate enrobed truffles) is far too involved to get into here - feel free to use the recipes below for the centers, and research tempering online!

"Stuff to Roll Them In"

Cocoa powder, coconut flakes, finely chopped nuts, and powdered sugar are all traditional options.. but feel free to go a bit crazy with it. Just be sure that whatever you use is either powdered, or finely chopped.

Dried fruit: Finely chop or process very dry fruit - chewy varieties don't work as well. If your local grocery store doesn't have a large variety, try dehydrating fresh fruit yourself! Additionally, chewy varieties of store-bought dehydrated fruit can usually be tossed into a food dehydrator for a day or two to achieve a dried texture. Freeze dried fruit is a great option that is readily available for order from online companies - pulverize them to a powder for a unique coating!

- Enhance cocoa powder or powdered sugar with the addition of various spices - cinnamon, cardamom, nutmeg, even cayenne pepper... whatever you like. Try using finely powdered dried citrus peels, or a little dried botanicals - rose petals, lavender. Even matcha (green tea) powder mixed into powdered sugar!

- Fruit powders can be ordered online in various types (see "Resources" section!). Try rolling truffles in exotic powdered fruit such as acai, goji berries, or mangosteen - A little goes a long way! Experiment with amount of flavoring used in your cocoa powder or powdered sugar, have fun with it!

- Finely ground cookies of any variety can add an interesting flavor and texture to your truffles. Ginger snaps, Oreos, Nilla wafers, maple cookies.

- Unique coatings: Try crystallized ginger, maple sugar, crushed coffee beans, finely chopped chocolate, instant hot chocolate powder, crushed pralines, finely crushed pretzels, toffee... even potato chips!

As you can see, there are many, many options available for "stuff to roll your truffles in" - and yes, that's a technical term. :) Mix and match any of these ideas - or anything else you come up with - with the recipes and flavoring options for ganache centers... and the possibilities really are endless!

Chocolate Ganache

Chocolate ganache is quite easy to make, but there are a few basic principles to keep in mind:

1. Too much liquid will prevent your ganache from setting up enough to roll properly. Fairly straightforward rule, right? If this happens, try adding extra chocolate... or use your runny ganache as a chocolate fondue or sauce for ice cream!

2. Not all chocolate varieties are created equally. While this applies to flavor, texture, and overall quality, I'm actually talking about behavior. Dark chocolate requires more liquid than milk chocolate, which requires more liquid than white chocolate. Sugar free chocolate requires a smaller amount of liquid than other varieties of chocolate... this is why we have several "basic" recipes below. Please be sure to follow the basic instructions for the variety of chocolate you are using!

3. Water is chocolate's enemy. Be very careful to use a dry bowl, dry utensils, and to not allow any water to fall into your chocolate. Water causes melted chocolate to "seize". Seizing is when melted chocolate comes in contact with even the tiniest amount of water, and becomes grainy, clumpy, and unpleasant. For this reason, you should never use a lid when melting chocolate (condensation will occur, and drip in!), and you should always be careful when using a double boiler.

4. Fat amount is important. The fat content in the chocolate ganache contributes to the smoothness, and the ganache's ability to hold together. Using milk instead of heavy cream really isn't an option. Additionally, if a high percentage of the liquid is coming from a non-fatty source (liqueur, rather than cream), it's a good idea to add extra butter.

5. Liquid added to chocolate must be warm. Pretty basic rule - cold liquid added to melted chocolate will cause it to seize. Warm liquid will not - this is why it's important

to heat up the cream mixture before adding it to the chocolate. Do not skip this step!

6. Chocolate chips are just fine to use. Yes, I'm sure the purists just had a heart attack over that phrase... deal with it!

Chocolate chips are a highly unusual medium for truffle making, consistently being eschewed for bars of pure chocolate. The thing is, however, that not only are chocolate chips are easy to find, they lack the sticker shock that comes with the more traditional chocolate options. I find that this makes chocolate chips a far more accessible option for those who are new to making truffles. Not only that, but they can make a great product, too - only the most avid chocolate connoisseur can really tell the difference between truffles made with a high end bar of chocolate, and those made with a good brand of chocolate chips.

For that reason, I believe chocolate chips are a great way to get in to making truffles. I developed a series of recipes using chocolate chips! Anyone can make these truffles at home, with common ingredients, for only about $4.00/30 truffles. Far less scary of a commitment than the traditional approach! With all of that said... on to the recipes!

Basic Dark Chocolate Truffles

Good quality dark chocolate chips	12 oz	340 g
Heavy whipping cream	½ cup	125 ml
Liqueur of choice	1/4 cup	50 ml
Butter	2 Tbsp	30 ml
Sugar, optional	2 Tbsp	30 ml
Stuff to roll them in		

Place chocolate chips into a glass mixing bowl, and put aside.

In a small saucepan, combine heavy whipping cream, liqueur, butter , and sugar. Heat to a boil, remove from heat.

Pour hot cream mixture into bowl of chocolate chips. Let sit for 3-5 minutes. Starting in the middle of the bowl, slowly start stirring the chocolate and cream until all of the chocolate is melted and the cream has disappeared into it – it should be smooth.

Cover with plastic wrap, preferably resting right on top of the surface – this prevents a skin from forming while it cools. Chill in the fridge for at least an hour or two, until it's pretty solid. Once solid, scoop out small amounts (a teaspoon or two), and roll them into balls. Try to handle the chocolate as quickly as possible, or it will melt.

Once all of the ganache is rolled into balls: wash & dry hands, then roll ganache centers in whichever coating(s) you'd like. Store in an airtight container for up to 1 week.

Flavor Ideas:
Jagermeister or Whisky, rolled in cocoa powder
Chambord, rolled in crushed freeze-dried raspberries
Grand Marnier, rolled in cocoa and finely chopped dried orange peel
Sambuca, rolled in powdered sugar
Black walnut, rolled in chopped walnuts
Kahlua, rolled in smashed chocolate covered espresso beans
Ginger liqueur, rolled in powdered sugar & finely chopped candied ginger
Tequila, add zest of 1-2 limes to cream mixture.

Basic Milk Chocolate Truffles

Good quality milk chocolate chips	10 oz	275 g
Heavy whipping cream	1/4 cup	50 ml
Liqueur of Choice	1/4 cup	50 ml
Butter	2 Tbsp	30 ml
Stuff to roll them in		

Place chocolate chips into a glass mixing bowl, and put aside.

In a small saucepan, combine heavy whipping cream, liqueur, and butter. Heat to a boil, remove from heat. Pour hot cream mixture into bowl of chocolate chips. Let sit for 3-5 minutes. Starting in the middle of the bowl, slowly start stirring the chocolate and cream until all of the chocolate is melted and the cream has disappeared into it – it should be smooth.

Cover with plastic wrap, preferably resting right on top of the surface – this prevents a skin from forming while it cools. Chill in the fridge for at least an hour or two, until it's pretty solid. Once solid, scoop out small amounts (a teaspoon or two), and roll them into balls. Try to handle the chocolate as quickly as possible, or it will melt.

Once all of the ganache is rolled into balls: wash and dry hands, then roll ganache centers in whichever coating(s) you'd like. Store in an airtight container for up to 1 week.

Flavor Ideas:
Cream tequila (Raspberry, strawberry, etc), rolled in powdered sugar
Irish Cream, rolled in instant hot chocolate powder
Rum or Frangelico, rolled in chopped nuts
Malibu rum, rolled in coconut
Goldschlager .rolled in cocoa powder, sprinkled with finely cut gold leaf
Pear brandy and ½ tsp cardamom, rolled in cocoa powder
Chocolate stout, rolled in finely crushed pretzels
Creme de banane and rum (2 Tbsp each) for the liqueur, add 1 tsp cinnamon. Roll in finely chopped pecans.
Southern Comfort, rolled in finely chopped pecans or almonds

Basic Milk Chocolate Truffles

Basic White Chocolate Truffles

Good quality white chocolate chips	12 oz	340 g
Heavy whipping cream	3 Tbsp	45 ml
Liqueur of choice	3 Tbsp	45 ml
Butter	2 Tbsp	30 ml
Stuff to roll them in		

Place chocolate chips into a glass mixing bowl, and put aside.

In a small saucepan, combine heavy whipping cream, liqueur, and butter. Heat to a boil, remove from heat.

Pour hot cream mixture into bowl of chocolate chips. Let sit for 3-5 minutes. Starting in the middle of the bowl, slowly start stirring the chocolate and cream until all of the chocolate is melted and the cream has disappeared into it – it should be smooth.

Cover with plastic wrap, preferably resting right on top of the surface – this prevents a skin from forming while it cools. Chill in the fridge for at least an hour or two, until it's pretty solid. Once solid, scoop out small amounts (a teaspoon or two), and roll them into balls. Try to handle the chocolate as quickly as possible, or it will melt.

Once all of the ganache is rolled into balls: wash and dry hands, then roll ganache centers in whichever coating(s) you'd like. Store in an airtight container for up to 1 week.

Flavor ideas:

Creme de banane and Midori (1 ½ Tbsp each), rolled in coconut
Sambuca and creme de banane (1 ½ Tbsp each), rolled in powdered sugar
Chai creme liqueur, rolled in cinnamon spiced powdered sugar
Green tea liqueur, rolled in powdered sugar flavored with matcha powder
Chambord, rolled in grated white chocolate
Malibu rum, rolled in coconut
Grapefruit liqueur, rolled in powdered sugar & dried grapefruit zest
Limoncello rolled in powdered sugar
Key lime liqueur rolled in coconut

Basic Peanut Butter Chip Truffles

Reese peanut butter chips	12 oz	340 g
Heavy whipping cream	1/4 cup	50 ml
Liqueur of choice	1/4 cup	50 ml
Butter	2 Tbsp	30 ml
Stuff to roll them in		

Place chocolate chips into a glass mixing bowl, and put aside.

In a small saucepan, combine heavy whipping cream, liqueur, and butter. Heat to a boil, remove from heat. Pour hot cream mixture into bowl of chocolate chips. Let sit for 3-5 minutes. Starting in the middle of the bowl, slowly start stirring the chocolate and cream until all of the chocolate is melted and the cream has disappeared into it – it should be smooth.

Cover with plastic wrap, preferably resting right on top of the surface – this prevents a skin from forming while it cools. Chill in the fridge for at least an hour or two, until it's pretty solid. Once solid, scoop out small amounts (a teaspoon or two), and roll them into balls. Try to handle the chocolate as quickly as possible, or it will melt.

Once all of the ganache is rolled into balls: wash and dry hands, then roll ganache centers in whichever coating(s) you'd like. Store in an airtight container for up to 1 week.

Flavor ideas:

Creme de cacao
Creme de banane
Banana cream tequila
Strawberry / raspberry liqueur or grape schnapps - "Peanut Butter and Jelly" truffles!

Basic Sugar Free Chocolate Truffles

Hershey's Sugar Free chips *	8 oz	225 g
Heavy whipping cream	3 Tbsp	45 ml
Liqueur of choice	2 Tbsp	30 ml
Butter	2 Tbsp	30 ml
Stuff to roll them in		

Place chocolate chips into a glass mixing bowl, and put aside.

In a small saucepan, combine heavy whipping cream, liqueur, and butter. Heat to a boil, remove from heat. Pour hot cream mixture into bowl of chocolate chips. Let sit for 3-5 minutes. Starting in the middle of the bowl, slowly start stirring the chocolate and cream until all of the chocolate is melted and the cream has disappeared into it – it should be smooth.

Cover with plastic wrap, preferably resting right on top of the surface – this prevents a skin from forming while it cools. Chill in the fridge for at least an hour or two, until it's pretty solid. Once solid, scoop out small amounts (a teaspoon or two), and roll them into balls. Try to handle the chocolate as quickly as possible, or it will melt.

Once all of the ganache is rolled into balls: wash and dry hands, then roll ganache centers in whichever coating(s) you'd like. Store in an airtight container for up to 1 week

* Hershey's is the only brand I've experimented with. Chocolate is finicky, and due to formulation, I'd have to assume that sugar free chocolate is even more so. Go ahead and try this with other brands of sugar free chocolate, but you may find that you need more or less cream. If your ganache doesn't firm up, you have a great chocolate sauce! If it's too firm, remelt it and add a little warm cream to it.

Final carb count on these truffles will depend a lot on what you roll them in, nuts are a great option!

White Chocolate Almond Amaretto Truffles

White chocolate chips	12 oz	340 g
Heavy whipping cream	1/3 cup	75 ml
Amaretto	3 Tbsp	45 ml
Almond paste or almond butter	3 Tbsp	45 ml
Finely chopped almonds		

Place chocolate chips into a glass mixing bowl, and put aside.

In a small saucepan, combine heavy whipping cream, amaretto, and almond paste/butter. Stir well, making sure to fully break up and incorporate the almond paste/butter into the mix. Heat to a boil, remove from heat. Pour hot cream mixture into bowl of chocolate chips. Let sit for 3-5 minutes. Starting in the middle of the bowl, slowly start stirring the chocolate and cream until all of the chocolate is melted and the cream has disappeared into it – it should be smooth.

Cover with plastic wrap, preferably resting right on top of the surface – this prevents a skin from forming while it cools. Chill in the fridge for at least an hour or two, until it's pretty solid. Once solid, scoop out small amounts (a teaspoon or two), and roll them into balls. Try to handle the chocolate as quickly as possible, or it will melt.

Once all of the ganache is rolled into balls: wash and dry hands, then roll ganache centers in finely chopped almonds. Store in an airtight container for up to 1 week.

White Chocolate Almond Amaretto Truffles

Eggnog Truffles

Good quality white chocolate chips*	12 oz	340 g
Eggnog	3 Tbsp	45 ml
Rum	3 Tbsp	45 ml
Powdered sugar		
Nutmeg		

Place chocolate chips into a glass mixing bowl, and put aside.

In a small saucepan, combine egg nog, and rum. Heat to a boil, remove from heat. Pour hot cream mixture into bowl of chocolate chips. Let sit for 3-5 minutes. Starting in the middle of the bowl, slowly start stirring the chocolate and cream until all of the chocolate is melted and the cream has disappeared into it – it should be smooth.

Cover with plastic wrap, preferably resting right on top of the surface – this prevents a skin from forming while it cools. Chill in the fridge for at least an hour or two, until it's pretty solid. Once solid, scoop out small amounts (a teaspoon or two), and roll them into balls. Try to handle the chocolate as quickly as possible, or it will melt.

Once all of the ganache is rolled into balls: wash and dry hands, then roll ganache centers in powdered sugar. Store in an airtight container for up to 1 week. Lightly sprinkle nutmeg over truffles before serving.

* This recipe can be used for milk or dark chocolate as well - just be sure to follow the basic recipe for the type of chocolate you want, swapping heavy cream out for egg nog.

Rum Raisin Milk Chocolate Truffles

Raisins	1 cup	250 ml
Rum	½ cup	125 ml
Good quality milk chocolate chips	10 oz	275 g
Heavy whipping cream	1/4 cup	50 ml
Butter	2 Tbsp	30 ml
Cocoa powder		

In a small bowl, cover raisins with rum. Allow to soak for at least 3 hours.

Place chocolate chips into a glass mixing bowl, and put aside. Drain liquid from raisins, chop. In a small saucepan, combine raisins, heavy whipping cream, and butter. Heat to a boil, remove from heat.

Pour hot cream mixture into bowl of chocolate chips. Let sit for 3-5 minutes. Starting in the middle of the bowl, slowly start stirring the chocolate and cream until all of the chocolate is melted and the cream has disappeared into it – it should be smooth.

Cover with plastic wrap, preferably resting right on top of the surface – this prevents a skin from forming while it cools. Chill in the fridge for at least an hour or two, until it's pretty solid. Once solid, scoop out small amounts (a teaspoon or two), and roll them into balls. Try to handle the chocolate as quickly as possible, or it will melt.

Once all of the ganache is rolled into balls: wash and dry hands, then roll ganache centers in cocoa powder. Store in an airtight container for up to 1 week.

Dark Chocolate Mojito Truffles

Good quality dark chocolate chips	12 oz	375 g
Fresh mint leaves	1 cup	250 ml
Heavy whipping cream	½ cup	125 ml
Rum	½ cup	125 ml
Butter	2 Tbsp	30 ml
Fresh lime zest	2-3 tsp	10-15 ml
Stuff to roll them in		

Place chocolate chips into a glass mixing bowl, and put aside.

In a small saucepan, combine mint leaves, heavy whipping cream, rum, and butter . Heat to a simmer, remove from heat. Allow to steep for 10 minutes.

Strain out the mint leaves, return cream mixture to stove top. Heat just to a simmer, add lime zest, remove from heat.

Pour hot cream mixture into bowl of chocolate chips. Let sit for 3-5 minutes. Starting in the middle of the bowl, slowly start stirring the chocolate and cream until all of the chocolate is melted and the cream has disappeared into it – it should be smooth.

Cover with plastic wrap, preferably resting right on top of the surface – this prevents a skin from forming while it cools. Chill in the fridge for at least an hour or two, until it's pretty solid. Once solid, scoop out small amounts (a teaspoon or two), and roll them into balls. Try to handle the chocolate as quickly as possible, or it will melt.

Once all of the ganache is rolled into balls: wash and dry hands, then roll ganache centers in whichever coating(s) you'd like. Store in an airtight container for up to 1 week.

Hop Flavored Dark Chocolate Truffles

I created this recipe for my hop fanatic husband one fall, as he harvested his crop of home grown hops. I paired the hops with dark chocolate - and he adored the result!

Good quality dark chocolate chips	12 oz	340 g
Heavy whipping cream	3/4 cup	175 ml
Dried hop cones, crushed	6	6
Butter	2 Tbsp	30 ml
Sugar	2 Tbsp	30 ml
Cocoa – We used Hershey's Special Dark		

Place chocolate chips into a glass mixing bowl, and set aside. On stovetop, bring heavy whipping cream, hop cones, and butter to a light simmer. Remove from heat, allow to steep for 10 minutes. Once steeping time is complete, bring to just a simmer again. Strain hot cream mixture into bowl of chocolate chips, discarding hop cones/leaves. Let sit for 3-5 minutes. Starting in the middle of the bowl, slowly start stirring the chocolate and cream until all of the chocolate is melted the cream disappeared into it – it should be smooth.

Cover with plastic wrap, preferably resting right on top of the surface – this prevents a skin from forming while it cools. Chill in the fridge for at least an hour or two, until it's pretty solid. Once solid, scoop out small balls (a teaspoon or so), and roll them into balls. Try to handle the chocolate as quickly as possible, or it will melt. Then, roll them in cocoa and eat them!

* Hops can vary wildly in size and flavor. Be sure to taste as you go – you may not want to use the whole 10 minute steeping time. If you don't have access to whole dried hop cones, you can use 1/4 tsp – 1/2 tsp of hop pellets! It doesn't take much, so your next batch of homebrew won't miss it!

Cream Puffs

Cream puffs are a great "fancy" dessert option. Not only are they insanely easy to make, they take very little in the way of ingredients, and can be customized many ways.

Cream puffs start out with the batter - Pâte à choux, or "choux pastry". It's a basic recipe that's used to make everything from cream puffs and eclairs to cruellers and churros. It doesn't contain any leavening ingredients (yeast, baking powder, baking soda, etc), instead relying on its high moisture content to puff during baking. Baked at a high temperature, the water becomes steam and creates large air pockets in the final product.

While this recipe itself isn't flavored with alcohol, it does provide an excellent serving vehicle for many of the other recipes in the book - the pastry creams, puddings, mousses, etc.

Pâte à choux

Water	1 cup	250 ml
Butter	½ cup	125 ml
Sugar	1 tsp	5 ml
Salt	½ tsp	2 ml
Flour	1 cup	250 ml
Large eggs	3	3
Egg whites	2	2

Preheat oven to 425°F (220°C). Line a baking sheet with parchment paper or a nonstick baking sheet. It's very important to not grease the pan - it will cause the pastries to flatten!

Combine water, butter, sugar, and salt in a medium sauce pan, heat to a boil. Remove from heat, add flour, stirring until well incorporated. Reduce heat to medium, return saucepan to stove top. Cook for another minute or so, until the dough comes together, leaving the sides of the pan. Transfer dough to the bowl of your mixer. Using the paddle attachment, beat the dough for a minute or so to allow it to cool slightly.

Meanwhile, beat together eggs and egg whites in a small bowl. With the mixer set to medium, add egg mixture to dough a little at a time, allowing eggs to fully incorporate into the dough before adding more. It may look like a separating mess, but I promise it will come together!

When all of the eggs are incorporated and the dough is smooth and shiny, it's ready to pipe! It'll be soft and a bit sticky, but more or less be able to hold it's shape. Pipe it out according to your desired use (below), and bake for the time indicated.

Cream Puffs:

Using a pastry bag with a medium/ large round or star tip, pipe out rounds that are about 2-2.5" in diameter and 1 ½" tall, leaving 2-3" between mounds.. Use a moistened finger to pat down any peaks of dough that may form as you finish piping each.

Bake for 12 minutes, then -WITHOUT opening the oven door - turn the temperature down to 350°F (180°C) and bake for another 35 minutes. Crack the oven door open a few inches, turn the heat off, and allow the puffs to cool in the oven for 30 minutes. This step allows the insides to dry out, providing a stronger structure to prevent collapse.

Once puffs are completely cool, cut in half horizontally, and fill with your choice of pastry cream, pudding, or mousse. Dust with powdered sugar, drizzle with chocolate, and/or serve with fresh fruit or berries!

Profiteroles:

Using spoons or a pastry bags, make tablespoon-sized mounds of batter, leaving 2" of space between each. Use a moistened finger to pat down any peaks of dough that may form as you finish piping each.

Bake for 12 minutes, then -WITHOUT opening the oven door - turn the temperature down to 350°F (180°C) and bake for another 25 minutes. Crack the oven door open a few inches, turn the heat off, and allow the puffs to cool in the oven for 30 minutes. This step allows the insides to dry out, providing a stronger structure to prevent collapse.

Fill a pastry bag with your choice of pastry cream, pudding, or mousse. Once puffs are completely cool, jam the tip of the pastry bag into the side of a puff, and fill! Dust with powdered sugar, drizzle with chocolate, and/or serve with fresh fruit or berries. Can also be used to make croquembouche. (Recipes on pages 119 and 120)

Eclairs:

Using a pastry bag with a large round or star tip, pipe out logs that are about 2" x 5-6" leaving 2" between logs. Use a moistened finger to pat down any peaks of dough that may form as you finish piping each.

Bake for 12 minutes, then -WITHOUT opening the oven door - turn the temperature down to 350°F (180°C) and bake for another 30 minutes. Crack the oven door open a few inches, turn the heat off, and allow the puffs to cool in the oven for 30 minutes. This step allows the insides to dry out, providing a stronger structure to prevent collapse.

Once logs are completely cool, cut in half horizontally, and fill with your choice of pastry cream, pudding, or mousse. Dip the tops in chocolate glaze (Recipe on page 119), chill.

Mini Eclairs:

Using a pastry bag with a medium/ large round or star tip, pipe out logs that are about 1" x 2" leaving 2" between logs. Use a moistened finger to pat down any peaks of dough that may form as you finish piping each.

Bake for 12 minutes, then -WITHOUT opening the oven door - turn the temperature down to 350°F (180°C) and bake for another 20 minutes. Crack the oven door open a few inches, turn the heat off, and allow the puffs to cool in the oven for 30 minutes. This step allows the insides to dry out, providing a stronger structure to prevent collapse.

Fill a pastry bag with your choice of pastry cream, pudding, or mousse. Once puffs are completely cool, jam the tip of the pastry bag into the side of a puff, and fill! Dip the tops in chocolate glaze (recipe below), chill.

Chocolate Glaze

Semi sweet chocolate	4 oz	125 g
Heavy cream	½ cup	125 ml

Finely chop chocolate, place into a glass mixing bowl, and put aside. In a small saucepan, heat heavy cream to a boil, remove from heat. Pour hot cream into the bowl of chocolate. Let sit for 3-5 minutes. Starting in the middle of the bowl, slowly start stirring the chocolate and cream until all of the chocolate is melted and the cream has disappeared into it – it should be smooth.

Glaze can be made a day or two in advance and kept - covered - in the refrigerator. Warm in the microwave for 20-30 seconds when ready to use.

Individual Chocolate Croquembouche

1 batch profiteroles, chilled		
Chocolate of choice	10 oz	275 g

Finely chop the chocolate (if not using chocolate chips), place in a microwave safe glass dish. Microwave on high for 20 seconds at a time until about half melted. Stir until completely melted. Divide profiteroles between number of servings needed. Ideally, you'll want 8, but that will vary greatly based on how large you made them! Assuming 8 small puffs, assemble them like this:

Dip the bottom of a cream puff in chocolate, place on small serving plate. Repeat with 3 more puffs, forming a square. You'll be using the melted chocolate to "glue" the profiteroles to the plate - and to each other as you go. Dip the bottoms of 3 more puffs into chocolate, arranging on top of the first 4 puffs. Top with 1 more dipped profiterole, to form a pyramid shape. Repeat with remaining servings, chill until chocolate sets up hard - at least 30 minutes.

To serve, drizzle with more chocolate, dust with powdered sugar, or pipe on some whipped cream. This is best served the same day - otherwise, the puffs can get soggy.

Traditional Croquembouche

This is a spectacular dessert. It's traditionally served at weddings in various European cities, but is also becoming a popular alternative to wedding cakes here in North America. It's also great for holiday dinners, or fancier potlucks.

A bit of a disclaimer here: This is an easy recipe to make, however, it's also sort of dangerous. I won't kid you, there is nothing worse than a hot sugar burn. If you drop the sugar onto skin, it will burn, it will stick, and it will HURT! Please exercise caution when dealing with the caramel in this recipe. If you do make this for a group, and you do manage to burn yourself in the process.. I promise the reception it will receive - and the amount of brownie points you'll gain - will be worth it. Be careful anyways, though.

2-3 batches of profiteroles, chilled		
Sugar	2 ½ cups	625 ml
Water	2/3 cup	150 ml

In a medium saucepan combine sugar and water, bringing to a boil over high heat. As soon as sugar begins to change color - about 300°F (150°C) - remove pan from heat. Set pan in a larger pan of warm water, on heat proof surface. This will slow the cooking, but keep the caramel warm enough to work with.

Work quickly to assemble your croquembouche. I like to freestyle it, not bothering with a form, but your mileage may vary. Feel free to use a styrofoam cone - like a craft store Christmas tree form - covered in parchment paper if you'd like.

Carefully dip a profiterole into the hot caramel, place on serving plate. Repeat with 15-20 more puffs to form a large circle. Make a second row on top of it, using less puffs and attaching them slightly to the inside of the first row. Continue making gradually smaller rings, until closing off the top with a single profiterole. Depending on how generous you are with the dipping, you may want to make a second batch of caramel at some point. When your tower is assembled, drizzle caramel or melted chocolate all over it, dust with powdered sugar, and/or garnish with decorative items such as candied flowers, nuts, etc.

If you're feeling adventurous, you can try making a web of sugar strands around it. Cut the very end off a wire whisk, or use 2-3 forks held together. Dip the tines of the forks / whisk into the remaining hot caramel, and use a swift motion to spin trails of caramel around the croquembouche. You can spin as much or as little sugar as you'd like, to achieve your desired effect.

Serve within 2 hours of making. It's best to serve ASAP, as the caramel threads (if used) are very sensitive to moisture in the air - and in the dessert itself - and will melt.

Traditional Croquembouche

Tuiles

A tuile is a light, crispy cookie that is used for anything from a garnish to a serving method. Much like the pâte à choux recipe, it's another of the few recipes in this book that doesn't include liqueur as flavoring. Tuiles are a great way to present other desserts, however - and will really kick up the presentation of pastry cream, pudding, mousses, and more!

Flour	1/3 cup	75 ml
Sugar	½ cup	125 ml
Salt	1 pinch	1 pinch
Large egg whites	3	3
Butter, melted	2 ½ Tbsp	37 ml
Fresh citrus zest (optional)	1 tsp	5 ml

In a small mixing bowl, combine flour, sugar, salt and egg whites. Whisk until combined, add melted butter (and zest, if using), and stir until just incorporated - do not over mix! Cover with plastic wrap, refrigerate for 30 minutes.

Preheat oven to 350°F (180°C). Line baking sheets with parchment paper or silicone baking mat, grease with cooking spray.

Scoop small mounds - about 2 Tbsp (30 ml) of batter - onto the sheets, 3 mounds per sheet. Spread each cookie into a 3" round using a wet finger, being careful to spread dough to an even thickness - the edges shouldn't be any thinner than the center. These will spread, so you really don't want to do any more than 3 per sheet.

Bake for 9-11 minutes, until edges are golden brown. Remove from oven, allow to cool for a 30 seconds or so, and quickly shape as desired (See below). Cookies should be used within a day or two, as they tend to lose their crispiness. Fill with pastry cream, mousse, pudding, marinated fresh fruit, or whatever else you want. Serve immediately.

Serving Suggestions:

- Separate a small amount of the batter, color with a small amount of cocoa powder or food coloring. Pipe decorations on to spread out cookie batter before baking.

- Roll into cone shapes by using a cornet mold. (A metal cone). Bake for an additional 3 minutes to set the cookie's shape up.

- Drape and shape warm cookies over upside-down bowls, glasses, ramekins, etc to create fancy serving bowls. Allow to cool completely before removing.

- Drape warm cookies over rolling pins or the sides of classes to create c -shaped serving baskets. Allow to cool completely before removing.

- Wrap various kitchen "tubes" with parchment paper. Think spice jars, Collins glasses, etc. Long, straight necked bottles of rum work great for this! Roll warm cookies around these tubes and allow to cool completely for a tuile-based cannoli shell! Pipe mousse in for a filling.

- Dip the edges of fully cooled baskets, bowls, and "cannoli" in melted chocolate. Optional: After dipping into chocolate, dip again into finely chopped coconut, nuts, or even cupcake sprinkles!

Jalapeno Beer Baklava

I know this sounds crazy, but it's really, really tasty. I personally don't even like beer, but love this funky new version of baklava! The jalapenos give a slight kick of flavor, but not an unmanageable or unpleasant amount of heat. This is still very much a sweet dessert!

Between the honey sauce and the filling, baklava is a dessert that lends itself well to experimentation. Ok, purists will argue that these aren't actually baklava... but whatever they are, they're tasty and impressive desserts. Much easier to make than one would assume, as well.

1 package phyllo sheets, thawed	1 lb	500 g
Finely chopped nuts *	1 lb	500 g
Butter, melted	1 cup	250 ml
Beer *	1 1/4 cups	300 ml
Jalapeno peppers	1-3	1-3
Sugar	1 cup	250 ml
Honey	½ cup	125 ml

Preheat oven to 350°F (180°C). Generously grease the bottoms and sides of a 9 x 13 inch pan.

Carefully unroll phyllo dough. Use a knife to slice the whole stack in half to make two stacks of 9 x 13" sheets. Cover with a damp cloth to prevent phyllo from drying out as you work - it's finicky, fragile stuff!

Lay two sheets of phyllo in bottom of prepared pan. Use a pastry brush to apply a thorough coating of melted butter. Layer with two more sheets. Repeat twice more, for a total of 8 sheets. Sprinkle 1/4 cup (50 ml) of the nuts evenly across the top. Layer with two more sheets, butter, and 1/4 cup (50 ml) nuts. Continue this pattern of two sheets, butter, nuts until you have about 6 sheets left. Layer two sheets, spread with butter, lay down two more sheets, spread with butter, and top with a final two sheets.

Use a sharp serrated knife to cut the baklava into diamond or square shapes, whatever size you'd like them. Be sure not to cut all the way to the bottom - cut to about 1/4 - ½" from the bottom. Bake for 45-55 minutes, until crisp and golden brown. In the meantime, make the sauce.

Finely chop jalapeno peppers. Remove seeds and rib meat if you prefer - leaving them in adds heat. Combine with beer in a small saucepan. Heat over medium until simmering, then turn heat down to low. Simmer for 5-10 minutes to infuse flavor. (5 for less peppery, 10 for more peppery!).

Add sugar to beer and pepper mixture, stir until dissolved. Add in honey, stir well, and simmer on medium-low for another 20 minutes.

When baklava has finished baking, remove from oven and immediately pour the honey beer sauce evenly over the top. Let cool completely before cutting all the way through to the bottom, using the precut lines.

* Use whatever nuts you like. I like roasted peanuts and/or cashews when using beer and jalapenos, but any nuts will work. As for beer, I like using a pale lager for this recipe, such as Corona. Anything too dark would overpower the other, more delicate flavors in this recipe - the honey, nuts, etc.

Jalapeno Beer Baklava

Other Boozy Baklava Flavor Ideas:

Tequila Lime: Use a blend of cashews and macadamia nuts for the filling. Omit jalapenos and beer. Simmer ½ cup (125 ml) water , ½ cup (125 ml) tequila, and the juice & zest of one lime with the sugar and honey.

Citrus & Cashew: Use cashews for the nuts. Omit jalapenos and beer, simmer ½ cup (125 ml) mead, ½ cup (125 ml) orange juice and the zest of 1 lemon with the sugar and honey.

Chocolate Jagermeister: Use a processor to finely chop 1 cup of dark chocolate chips. Mix with 1 cup finely chopped almonds, use this for the nut mix. Omit jalapenos and beer. Simmer ½ cup (125 ml) water and ½ cup (125 ml) Jagermeister with the sugar and honey.

Cranberry & Pomegranate: Use 1 cup of finely chopped sweetened dried cranberries and 2 cups of thinly sliced almonds for the nuts mixture. Omit jalapenos and beer. Simmer ½ cup (125 ml) water, ½ cup (125 ml) Pama Pomegranate liqueur, and the zest of 1 orange with the sugar and honey.

Soufflé

Soufflé is one of those dishes that terrifies some home cooks. So many stories out there about how difficult they are to make, how easily they fall... whatever. It's not as difficult as you've heard! Here is an easy recipe that anyone can make at home.

As with all recipes that rely on whipped egg whites for structure, the key is to have an incredibly clean mixer bowl - and whisk attachment - and to not allow even a speck of egg yolk into the whites to be whipped. Any fat at all - whether residue on the bowl, or from stray bits of egg yolk - will prevent the egg whites from properly whipping up. While these are a great finale to any dinner, be advised - these need to be served immediately upon being removed from the oven, or they'll deflate. Time your meal well!

Individual Boozy Soufflé

Butter	1/4 cup	50 ml
Sugar	1/4 cup	50 ml
Large egg yolks	4	4
Sugar	½ cup	125 ml
Liqueur of choice*	4 Tbsp	60 ml
Large egg whites	6	6
Cream of tartar	1/4 tsp	1 ml
Salt	1 pinch	1 pinch
Powdered Sugar (optional)		
Sauce, recipe follows (optional)		

Preheat oven to 400°F (200°C), position a heavy baking sheet on the middle rack. Grease 6 (8 oz / 1 cup / 250 ml) ramekins with butter. Divide 1/4 cup of sugar between them, turning to coat evenly. Set aside.

Combine egg yolks and 1/4 cup (50 ml) of the sugar in a bowl. Beat with an electric mixer until light, fluffy, and pale yellow. Add in liqueur, stir until fully incorporated and smooth.

In stand mixer, whip egg whites at high speed until light and foamy. Add in cream of tartar and salt, continue whipping until soft peaks form. Slowly add the remaining 1/4 cup (50 ml) of sugar, a little at a time, until fully incorporated. Continue whipping until stiff peaks form. Carefully fold the boozy egg yolks mixture into the whipped egg whites, divide evenly between the prepared dishes. Gently transfer ramekins to the baking sheet in the oven. Bake for 10-12 minutes, or until golden brown on top. Souffles will have risen up to 2" above the edge of the ramekin! Dust with powdered sugar or drizzle with sauce of your choice. Serve immediately.

* Grand Marnier is a popular choice, but feel free to experiment! Almost any non-cream liqueur that you like to drink would work well with this recipe!

Individual Boozy Chocolate Soufflé

Butter	1/4 cup	50 ml
Sugar	1/4 cup	50 ml
Heavy Cream	1/4 cup	50 ml
Liqueur of choice	1/4 cup	50 ml
Butter	3 Tbsp	45 ml
Chocolate (70%+ cacao), chopped	12 oz	340 g
Large Eggs, separated	6	6
Sugar	½ cup	125 ml
Cream of tartar	1/4 tsp	1 ml
Salt	1 pinch	1 pinch

Powdered Sugar (optional)
Sauce, recipe follows (optional)

Preheat oven to 400°F (200°C), position a heavy baking sheet on the middle rack. Grease 6 (8 oz / 1 cup/250 ml) ramekins with butter. Divide 1/4 cup (50 ml) of sugar between them, turning to coat evenly. Set aside.

In a small saucepan, combine heavy whipping cream, liqueur, and butter. Heat to a boil, remove from heat. Pour hot cream mixture into bowl of chocolate, let sit for 3-5 minutes. Starting in the middle of the bowl, slowly start stirring the chocolate and cream until all of the chocolate is melted and the cream has disappeared into it – it should be smooth. Allow to cool to room temperature.

Combine egg yolks and 1/4 cup (50 ml) of the sugar in a bowl. Beat with an electric mixer until light, fluffy, and pale yellow. Pour in the cooled chocolate mixture, beat until everything is fully incorporated and smooth.

In stand mixer, whip egg whites at high speed until light and foamy. Add in cream of tartar and salt, continue whipping until soft peaks form. Slowly add the remaining 1/4 cup (50 ml) of sugar, a little at a time, until fully incorporated. Continue whipping until stiff peaks form.

Carefully fold the chocolate egg yolk mixture into the whipped egg whites, divide evenly between the prepared dishes.

Carefully transfer ramekins to the baking sheet in the oven. Bake for 10-12 minutes, or until golden brown on top. Souffles will have risen up to 2" above the edge of the ramekin!

Dust with powdered sugar or drizzle with sauce of your choice. Serve immediately.

Boozy Sauce for Soufflé:

Egg yolk	1	1
Heavy cream	1/4 cup	50 ml
Liqueur of choice	1/4 cup	50 ml

Combine ingredients in a small saucepan, stirring until smooth. Bring to a gentle simmer over low heat, stirring until mixture reaches desired thickness. Serve over Soufflé.

Dessert Ravioli

There are so many different ways to make a traditional dinner favorite - ravioli - into a new dessert favorite. Dough and filling types can be mixed and matched, cooking method can vary - baked, boiled, deep fried - and sauces can be used. Dessert ravioli can be a little more labor intensive than some other recipes, but the effort is worth it! Dessert ravioli is something unique and unexpected. With a little creativity in presentation, it can really be a showstopper for your guests! Try serving it in martini glasses, with a light drizzling of sauce.

Basic Dessert Ravioli

Flour	2 2/3 cups	650 ml
Large eggs	3	3
Water	1/3 cup	75 ml
Filling, recipes follow		

Combine flour and eggs in food processor until fully incorporated. Slowly stream 1/3 cup (75 ml) water into the mix - while running - until dough comes together. You may not need the whole amount of water. Knead dough until smooth, wrap tightly in plastic wrap, allow to rest for 1 hour.

Roll dough as thin as possible - about 1/16" of an inch. Having a pasta machine for this is handy, but it can be rolled with a rolling pin... and a bit of patience! Use a round cookie cutter or rim of a glass - 2.5 - 3" or so - to cut rounds from the dough. Mound 1-2 tsp (5-10 ml)of filling into
the middle of a round, top with another round. Carefully seal the edges by running a wet finger around the inner edge of a round, then pinching the edges together around the entire seam. Alternatively, use a ravioli or pierogi maker.

Bring a large pot of water to a boil. Gently add ravioli to boiling water, one at a time, about 6 to a batch. Ravioli has finished cooking when they float to the surface of the water. Use a slotted spoon to remove cooked ravioli from the water, dip in cool water to halt the cooking process.   Serve warm or cold, dusted with powdered sugar or drizzled with sauce of your choice.

Chocolate Dessert Ravioli

Flour	2 1/3 cups	575 ml
Cocoa powder	½ cup	125 ml
Large eggs	3	3
Water	1/3 cup	75
Filling, recipes follow		

Combine flour, cocoa and eggs in food processor until fully incorporated. Slowly stream 1/3 cup (75 ml) water into the mix - while running - until dough comes together. You may not need the whole amount of water. Knead dough until smooth, wrap tightly in plastic wrap, allow to rest for 1 hour.

Roll dough as thin as possible - about 1/16" of an inch. Having a pasta machine for this is handy, but it can be rolled with a rolling pin... and a bit of patience! Use a round cookie cutter or rim of a glass - 2.5 - 3" or so - to cut rounds from the dough. Mound 1-2 tsp (5-10 ml)of filling into the middle of a round, top with another round. Carefully seal the edges by running a wet finger around the inner edge of a round, then pinching the edges together around the entire seam. Alternatively, use a ravioli or pierogi maker.

Bring a large pot of water to a boil. Gently add ravioli to boiling water, one at a time, about 6 to a batch. Ravioli has finished cooking when they float to the surface of the water. Use a slotted spoon to remove cooked ravioli from the water, dip in cool water to halt the cooking process.   Serve warm or cold, dusted with powdered sugar or drizzled with sauce of your choice.

Chocolate Dessert Ravioli with Cream Liqueur Sauce

Fried Dessert Ravioli

Wonton wrappers	1 package	1 package
Large egg, beaten	1	1
Filling, recipes follow		
Vegetable oil for frying.		

Heat oil in a deep fryer or heavy bottomed large frying pan to 350°F (180°C).

Lay individual wonton wrappers out on flat work surface. Lightly brush the edges of each wrapper with beaten egg. Place 1 Tbsp filling in the middle of each wonton wrapper. Fold each wrapper along the diagonal, creating a triangle shaped pocket. Press the edges together to seal, working out any extra air as you go along.

Carefully add ravioli to hot oil, working in batches. Cook for about 1 minute on each side, or until golden brown. Use a slotted spoon to remove cooked ravioli from the deep fryer, place on paper towels to drain excess oil. Serve warm, dusted with powdered sugar or drizzled with sauce of your choice.

Cheese Filling for Dessert Ravioli

Ricotta cheese, well drained	1 ½ cups	375 ml
Sugar	1/4 cup	50 ml
Large Egg	1	1
Liqueur of choice	1 Tbsp	15 ml

Combine ingredients, stirring till well incorporated. Chill until use.

Chocolate Filling for Dessert Ravioli

Use any of the chocolate truffle recipes, starting on page 105. Follow recipe up until truffles are rolled. Roll as described, but do not use any of the coatings.

Freeze ganache balls for 30 minutes, then use as filling for any of the ravioli recipes. Ganache will soften/melt as the ravioli cooks - best served warm.

Bananas Foster Filling for Dessert Ravioli

Just-ripe bananas	2	2
Pecans, finely chopped	1 Tbsp	15 ml
Brown sugar	1/4 cup	50 ml
Rum	2 Tbsp	30 ml
Creme de banane	1 Tbsp	15 ml
Cinnamon	1 tsp	5 ml
Corn starch	1 Tbsp	15 ml

Mash bananas, combine with pecans, set aside

In a medium saucepan, combine remaining ingredients, stir until well incorporated. Add in banana mixture, bring to a simmer over medium low heat. Cook, stirring constantly, until quite thick. Remove from heat, allow to cool to room temperature. Chill until use.

Berry Filling for Dessert Ravioli

Liqueur of choice	1 Tbsp	15 ml
Corn starch	2 Tbsp	30 ml
Fresh berries, mashed	½ cup	125 ml
Ricotta cheese, well drained	1 cup	250 ml
Sugar	1/4 cup	50 ml
Large Egg	1	1

In a small saucepan, combine corn starch and liqueur together to make a smooth paste. Add mashed berries, bring to a simmer on medium-low heat. Cook and stir until thickened, about 3 minutes. Remove from heat, allow to cool. Add ricotta cheese, sugar, and egg to berry mixture, stir until well incorporated. Chill until use.

Boozy Berry Sauce

Liqueur of choice*	½ cup	125 ml
Water	½ cup	125 ml
Berries *	3 cups	750 ml
Cornstarch	1 - 2 Tbsp	15-30 ml
Water	1 Tbsp	15 ml

Combine water, sugar, and berries together in a medium saucepan. Bring just to a boil, reduce heat and simmer for 7 minutes.

In a small bowl, stir cornstarch and water together to form a smooth, thick paste. 1 Tbsp will yield a runnier sauce, while 2 Tbsp will create a thicker sauce - go with whichever you prefer! Carefully pour this paste into the berry mixture, stir to incorporate fully. Bring fruit mixture back up to a simmer, allow to cook for another 2-3 minutes, or until desired consistency.

* Almost any fruity liqueur would work. This sauce is especially good with Grand Marnier, Chambord, or Limoncello. As for berries, use any you'd like - solo or in combination with other berries.

Cream Liqueur Sauce

The sauce pictured on page 129 was made with Kahlua, but you can use almost any liqueur you like.

Cornstarch	1 Tbsp	15 ml
Granulated sugar	1/4 cup	50 ml
Heavy whipping cream	2/3 cup	150 ml
Liqueur of choice	1/3 cup	75 ml

In a small saucepan, whisk together corn starch and sugar until well combined. Add heavy whipping cream and continue whisking until well combined and smooth.

Bring to a simmer over medium heat, stirring frequently until mixture thickens. Remove from heat, whisk in liqueur. Use warm or cold.

Other sauce ideas for Dessert Ravioli:

- Basic bread pudding boozy sauce (Page 89)
- White chocolate amaretto sauce (Page 92)
- Any of the truffle ganaches (Starting on page 105), served warm!

Flavor Ideas:

Chocolate ravioli with cheese filling and berry sauce. Try Grand Marnier in both the filling and sauce! Also great - creme de cacao in filling, with a Chambord / raspberry sauce

Basic or deep fried ravioli with bananas foster filling and chocolate sauce (use rum to flavor!). Sprinkle chopped pecans over dessert just before serving!

Chocolate overload - chocolate ravioli with chocolate filling and chocolate sauce!

Boozy Madeleines

Madeleines are a traditional tea cake - almost a cookie - from northeastern France. While there are several different variants of flavor for the cakes, one thing is pretty much constant - the shape. Madeleines are baked using a special pan with shallow, shell shaped indentations. Very pretty! Madeleine pans can be purchased at many department and home goods stores, or online. (See resources page!)

Traditional Madeleines are great as is... but the addition of a citrusy liqueur kicks it up a notch. Try this with Limoncello, Grand Marnier, even Triple Sec for a new take on a classic! Alternatively, try omitting the zest and liqueur, and using 1-2 tsp of homemade flavor extract. Such a simple, elegant treat... but the possibilities are endless!

Cake flour	1 ½ cups	375 ml
Baking powder	2 tsp	10 ml
Large eggs	5	5
Sugar	1 cup	250 ml
Butter, melted	½ cup	125 ml
Liqueur of choice	1 tbsp	15 ml
Zest of 1 lemon		
Powdered sugar, optional		
Chocolate, optional		

Preheat oven to 400°F (200°C). Generously grease Madeleine pan with shortening. Sift flour and baking powder together into a bowl, set aside.

Combine eggs and sugar, beat until very pale yellow. Add butter, liqueur, and lemon zest, mix until well combined. Add dry ingredients to mixing bowl of wet ingredients, stir until well incorporated and smooth.

Spoon 1 Tbsp (15 ml) of batter into each prepared Madeleine mold cavity. Bake for 10-12 minutes, or until golden. Turn Madeleines out onto a clean dishtowel, cool.

To serve, dust Madeleines with a little powdered sugar, or dip 1 end/side of each shell into melted chocolate.

Stuffed Strawberries

Stuffed strawberries are so easy to make, but are an elegant crowd pleaser! These are also great to make as a last minute treat for Valentine's Day, or any romantic dinner.

Large Strawberries	15 - 20	15-20
Cream cheese, softened	8 oz	225 g
Powdered sugar	½ cup	125 ml
Liqueur of choice	2 Tbsp	30 ml
- or -		
Homemade flavor extract	1-2 tsp	5-10 ml

Cut the tops off the strawberries, removing the hull (green stem, leaf, etc) and any white core that may be present.

Combine cream cheese, powdered sugar, and liqueur or flavor extract in the bowl of a stand mixer. Cream together until everything is fully incorporated and smooth.

Spoon cheese filling into a piping bag fitted with a medium star tip. Pipe mixture into each strawberry, arrange directly on to serving plate as you go.

Flavor & Serving Ideas:

- Grand Marnier is a traditional choice. Other citrus liqueurs like triple sec, Limoncello or even Blue Curacao would work well. Try adding a little citrus zest!

- Try substituting mascarpone cheese for the cream cheese, and use coffee liqueur for flavor. It's like tiramisu in a strawberry shell! Dust with a little cocoa for garnish.

- Try 1 Tbsp (15 ml) each rum and lime juice for a daiquiri strawberry!

- Stuffed strawberries can also be dipped in melted chocolate. Dip after hulling the strawberries, and allow the chocolate to harden before carefully filling with the cheese mixture.

Rum Runner Trifle

I am a big fan of Rum Runners - they're definitely up there among my favorite cocktails ever. I created this recipe a few years ago, as the weather turned from summer to fall.. and I realized that our summer had been lacking in the Rum Runners department.

This recipe seems involved, but it comes together quite easily! The cake should be made at least a day before serving, but can be made even further ahead than that! Feel free to tightly wrap the slab of cake in plastic wrap and freeze for a couple of weeks, allowing it to defrost for an hour or two before cutting it up.

While I like to make up my trifles fresh RIGHT before serving them, many people find that they get better by aging a day or two in the fridge – making them an excellent dessert for entertaining!

Cake:

Cake Flour	3 cups	750 ml
Sugar	2 1/4 cups	550 ml
Baking powder	2 Tbsp	30 ml
Salt	1 ½ tsp	7 ml
Instant vanilla pudding mix	3 ½ oz	96 g
Large Eggs	6	6
Amber rum	½ cup	125 ml
Orange juice	½ cup	125 ml
Pineapple juice	½ cup	125 ml
Butter, melted	1 ½ cups	375 ml
Pure vanilla extract	2 Tbsp	30 ml
Zest of 1 orange		

Banana Rum Soak, Pudding Mixture, Fruit (Following page)

Preheat oven to 350°F (180°C). Liberally a 9x 13" cake pan with vegetable shortening, and/or spray with baking spray.

Combine flour, sugar, baking powder, salt, and pudding mix in a large mixing bowl. Add in eggs, rum, and orange juice, beating until smooth. Carefully add melted butter, vanilla, and orange zest to the mix, mixing on medium speed until smooth.

Pour batter into prepared cake pan. Bake until golden and knife inserted into center of batter comes out clean – about 45 minutes. Allow to cool 10-15 minutes before turning cake out onto baking rack to cool fully. Ideally, allow to cool to room temperature, wrap tightly with plastic wrap.

Allow cake to sit overnight, assemble trifle the following day.

Banana Rum Soak

Light rum	1/4 cup	50 ml
Creme de banane liqueur	1/4 cup	50 ml
Sugar	½ cup	125 ml

Combine ingredients in a small saucepan, heat until sugar dissolves. Set aside.

Pudding Mixture*

2 boxes Instant vanilla pudding mix	7 oz	192 g
Milk	1 3/4 cups	425 ml
Blackberry brandy	1/4 cup	50 ml
Purple food coloring, optional		

Whisk together pudding mix, milk, blackberry brandy, and food coloring – if desired. Allow to set up slightly before assembling trifle.

Fruit

Bananas, sliced	7-8	7-8
Lemon juice	2 Tbsp	30 ml
Fresh blackberries	~ 3 cups	~ 750 ml
To Assemble Trifle		

Cut cake into 1- 1.5" cubes.

Slice bananas, gently toss with lemon juice to prevent browning

In a large trifle-type bowl, arrange 1/3 of the cake cubes (or whatever percentage it takes to get a good solid layer down) on the bottom. Drizzle with banana rum soak, spoon 1/3 of the blackberry pudding mixture evenly over top. Arrange banana slices and blackberries on top of pudding layer.

Repeat twice with remaining cake, binder, and fruit. Serve immediately, or cover with plastic wrap and refrigerate until serving.

* Feel free to substitute homemade custard from the "Creamy" chapter. That's how I tend to do it, but have utilized instant pudding mix in this recipe to keep things a bit more simple!

Rum Runner Trifle

Melon Ball Trifle

Much like the Rum Runner Trifle, this recipe seems involved ... but it comes together quite easily! The cake should be made at least a day before serving, but can be made even further ahead than that! Feel free to tightly wrap the slab of cake in plastic wrap and freeze for a couple of weeks, allowing it to defrost for an hour or two before cutting it up.

While I like to make up my trifles fresh RIGHT before serving them, many people find that they get better by aging a day or two in the fridge – making them an excellent dessert for entertaining. This is a fun, pretty, and tasty dessert – always a hit to bring to potlucks and special events!

Cake

Cake Flour	3 cups	750 ml
Sugar	2 1/4 cups	550 ml
Baking powder	2 Tbsp	30 ml
Salt	1 ½ tsp	7 ml
Instant vanilla pudding mix	3 ½ oz	96 g
Large Eggs	6	6
Vodka	½ cup	125 ml
Orange juice	1 cup	250 ml
Butter, melted	1 ½ cups	375 ml
Pure vanilla extract	2 Tbsp	30 ml
Zest of 1 orange		

Preheat oven to 350°F (180°C). Liberally a 9x 13" cake pan with vegetable shortening, and/or spray with baking spray

Combine flour, sugar, baking powder, salt, and pudding mix in a large mixing bowl. Add in eggs, vodka, and orange juice, beating until smooth. Carefully add melted butter, vanilla, and orange zest to the mix, mixing on medium speed until smooth.

Pour batter into prepared cake pan. Bake until golden and knife inserted into center of batter comes out clean – about 45 minutes. Allow to cool 10-15 minutes before turning cake out onto baking rack to cool fully. Ideally, allow to cool to room temperature, wrap tightly with plastic wrap. Allow cake to sit overnight, assemble trifle the following day.

Melon Soak

Water	1/4 cup	50 ml
Midori melon liqueur	1/4 cup	50 ml
Sugar	½ cup	125 ml

Combine ingredients in a small saucepan, heat until sugar dissolves. Set aside. (Alternatively: Substitute 1/4 cup reserved water/syrup from the canned mandarin orange slices for the plain water.

Pudding Mixture**

2 boxes Instant vanilla pudding mix	7 oz	192 g
Milk	1 3/4 cups	425 ml
Midori melon liqueur	1/4 cup	50 ml

Whisk together pudding mix, milk, melon liqueur, and food coloring – if desired. Allow to set up slightly before assembling trifle.

Fruit
2-3 cans mandarin orange segments, drained
1-2 honeydew melons

To Assemble Trifle

Cut cake into 1- 1.5" cubes.

Cut melons in half, scoop out and discard seeds. Slice, remove rind, and chop into bite sized pieces. (You can use a melon baller if you want to get fancy with it!)

In a large trifle-type bowl, arrange 1/3 of the cake cubes (or whatever percentage it takes to get a good solid layer down) on the bottom. Drizzle with Melon soak, spoon 1/3 of the pudding mixture evenly over top. Arrange orange segments and melon pieces on top of pudding layer.

Repeat twice with remaining cake, pudding, and fruit. Serve immediately, or cover with plastic wrap and refrigerate until serving.

* Feel free to substitute homemade custard from the "Creamy" chapter. That's how I tend to do it, but have utilized instant pudding mix in this recipe to keep things a bit more simple!

Homemade Wine Slush Mix

If you've ever been to a large trade show, home show ... chances are, you've seen a booth hawking wine slushie mixes. The samples are so good, it's easy to drop the $12 or so for the 12 oz baggie of powdered mix. Trust me, we've done so... twice. That second time, I took a look at the ingredients and almost had a heart attack. I couldn't believe what I'd just paid so MUCH for!

While we all loved the slush, I decided that I would set about to "reverse engineer" it. Between the ingredient listing, listed weight, nutritional info, and the unused second bag sitting in our liquor cabinet... I didn't figure it would be hard to do.

It wasn't. :)

The ingredients are simple, and the technique is one of those "so simple, it shouldn't be considered an actual recipe" deals. You, too, can make homemade wine slush mix at home! While matcha powder isn't cheap, this recipe doesn't take much at all – your wine slush mix should cost less than $1.50/batch!

Sugar*	1 2/3 - 1 3/4 cups	400 ml
Citric acid	1 ½ tsp	7 ml
Matcha (green tea) powder (optional)	1/4 tsp	1 ml

Measure all ingredients into a food processor. Run the food processor for a minute or two, to finely process the sugar and evenly distribute the ingredients.

Pour powdered mix into a baggie or airtight container until ready to use.

* Less for if using a sweeter wine, more for a dry wine

To make wine slush: Pour 1 batch of mix into a 1 gallon freezer bag (or large bowl). Add 1 750 ml bottle of wine, and 3 cups (750 ml) of water. Stir/shake well. Freeze for about 3 hours before serving in glasses of your choice.

(I like to freeze the mixture for a bit longer, stirring/shaking every 30 minutes or so, to produce a finer grained sorbet style dessert, pictured.)

As a Gift Idea: Package 1 batch of mix into a clear craft/goodie baggie, push most of the air out, and tie with a twist tie. Add a ribbon bow. Print the above directions ("To make wine slush") onto a pretty card and attach to the baggie or ribbon.

Want a fancier baggie, to double as gift itself? Check out Dragon Chow Dice Bags – they're big enough to hold a batch!

Variations:

"Sangria Slush" mix: Measure sugar and citric acid into food processor (skip the matcha powder). Zest one orange, one lemon, and one lime on top of the measured ingredients before processing.

Flavored Wine Slush Mixes: Measure sugar and citric acid into food processor (skip the matcha powder). Add flavoring of your choice: About 1 tsp of flavor extract, or ½ tsp of a flavor oil will do it, but feel free to flavor to your taste. Process as directed above. Spread mixture out on a cookie sheet and allow to dry for about an hour. Run dried mixture through the food processor to break up any dried clumps you may have, then store per main recipe.

When it comes to extracts or flavor oils, you can have fun with it, but you will want to label the flavor if giving it as a gift. Also, consider the wine to be used. Generally speaking, white wines will work better with flavored mixes than red will.

As an example, banana extract would make a fun slush, but would definitely be better with a white wine. Also, peach flavor oil, combined with a champagne would be very tasty – like a frozen peach bellini!

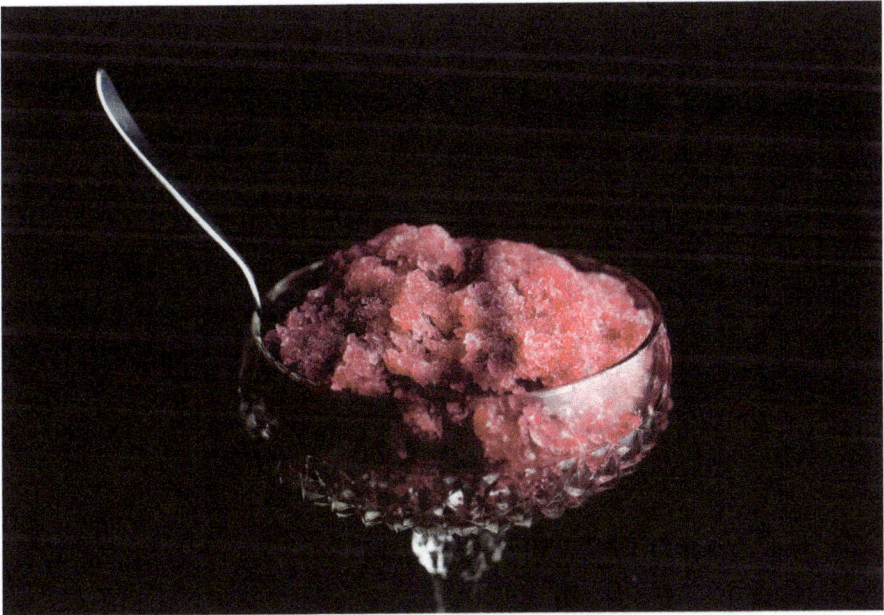

Homemade Wine Slush

Munchy

Sometimes, you're less worried about putting on a show, and just want yummy things to snack on. In this chapter, you'll find a variety of snack foods and casual desserts: cookies, candies, ice cream, and more!

Noelles

Growing up, Christmas meant that one of the aunts would be bringing the original version of these cookies to the festivities. Very addictive... Of course, I had to mess with it. Here is a more "grown up" version of my childhood favorite!

Butter	½ cup	125 ml
Sugar	½ cup	125 ml
Brown sugar	1/4 cup	50 ml
Large egg	1	1
Amaretto	1 Tbsp	15 ml
Flour	1 1/4 cup	300 ml
Baking powder	½ tsp	2 ml
Salt	½ tsp	2 ml
Dark chocolate chips	1 cup	250 ml
Coconut	3/4 cup	175 ml
Maraschino cherries, drained	3/4 cup	175 ml

Preheat oven to 350°F (180°C). Line 2 baking sheets with parchment paper.

Cream together butter and sugars until fluffy. Add in egg and amaretto, mix until well incorporated. In a separate bowl, combine flour, baking powder, and salt. Add to wet mixture, stir until fully incorporated and relatively smooth. Stir in chocolate chips, coconut, and cherries

Use a teaspoon to drop very generous - about 2 tsp - mounds onto cookie sheets. Bake for 12-15 minutes, or until starting to turn a light golden brown on top. (The edges will turn golden earlier than the top.) Makes about 24 cookies.

Noelles

Fruit Cake Cookies

Think you dislike fruitcake? Try these! A spiced brown sugar cookie, stuffed with candied cherries, pineapple, golden raisins... and a hint of Jack Daniels! (Also great for those who actually like fruitcake, of course!) The raisins need to soak overnight, so be sure to plan ahead to make these.

Golden raisins	2 ½ cups	625 ml
Jack Daniel's whisky	½ cup	125 ml
Butter	½ cup	125 ml
Brown sugar	½ cup	125 ml
Large eggs	3	3
Flour	1 ½ cup	375 ml
Baking soda	½ tsp	2 ml
Cinnamon	1 ½ tsp	7 ml
Nutmeg	½ tsp	2 ml
Ground cloves	½ tsp	2 ml
Salt	1/4 tsp	1 ml
Chopped pecans	3 ½ cups	875 ml
Mixed candied fruit*	1 ½ cups	375 ml

The night before baking, place raisins in a glass bowl, separating any clumps of raisins. Add whisky, stir slightly, cover and allow to soak overnight.

The next day, preheat oven to 325°F (160°C). Line baking sheets with parchment paper, or spray with cooking spray.

Cream together butter and brown sugar until fluffy. Add in eggs, mix until well incorporated. In a separate bowl, combine flour, baking soda, cinnamon, nutmeg, cloves, and salt. Add to wet mixture, stir until fully incorporated and relatively smooth.

Drain any remaining whisky from the soaking raisins. Stir raisins, pecans, and candied fruit into the wet mixture. The mixture will be VERY thick - I recommend using a study wooden or metal mixing spoon for this step.

Use a teaspoon to drop very generous - about 2 tsp - mounds onto cookie sheets. Bake for 18-20 minutes, or until golden brown. Allow to cool fully before storing in an airtight container

* You can buy candied fruit already mixed, or mix your own. Typically, candied green and red cherries, candied pineapple, and candied citrus peel are most popular, but you can also find candied pears, plums, and more, if desired. In some areas, these are referred to as "Glacé fruits".

Gluten Free Fruitcake Cookies

The fact that this recipe even exists… it's sort of a miracle. You see, I'm one of those people that hate fruitcake. It's not that I buy into mass "ew!" hysteria (I love broccoli and Brussels sprouts, for instance!), it's that I find glaceed / candied fruit to be one of the nastiest things on the planet. I mean, right up there with Velveeta. Gross.

Then, there is the "gluten free" issue. I am NOT a fan of anything that uses fake flours to make a regular recipe into a gluten free recipe. I'm a major "Gluten Free" Snob, and pretty much stick to treats that are inherently gluten free, such as coconut macaroons, Pavlova, and French Macarons. I've just always found anything made with the fake flours to be nasty, both in taste and texture.

You may be asking yourself, right about now, WHY I created this recipe. Well, I'll tell you – painkillers!

I really hate taking painkillers, as they make me feel really gross. I have to be in really rough shape to even consider it – but one weekend in 2011, I couldn't move my arm/shoulder without screaming pain for a few hours, I finally caved in. 45 minutes later, I was sorta woozy and craving fruitcake. Yes, I know – I *HATE* the stuff.

So, I did what one would expect an ADD, creative baker with gluten allergies to do when high as a kite – I designed a gluten free recipe, and demanded … err.. nicely asked my husband to drive me shopping for the ingredients I would require. I chopped the fruit and soaked them in booze overnight, looking forward to baking them the next day.

OH. WOW. These are amazing! I mean, amazing-amazing, not "amazing – for a gluten free cookie". The substitution of dried fruits for glaceed, the Southern Comfort… it just created this vivid palette of flavor, which *completely* hid any gluten-free nastiness! With so much texture from the fruit and nuts, the cookies COMPLETELY lack any of the weird texture issues I have with normal gluten free cookies.

These were so fabulous, my not-stuck-in-gluten-free-hell husband LOVES them. A few days later, and I'm already putting on a second batch! So good!

We used a mix of raisins, cranberries, cherries, apricots, and pineapple, but you can use a combination of whatever dried fruit you love. Oh, and don't worry about buying too much – not only will you want to put on another batch once you try these… but I'll be posting a recipe for gluten free fruitcake tomorrow!

(This makes about 20-24 LARGE cookies… probably a good idea to double the recipe!)

Mixed dried fruit	1 lb	500 g
Southern Comfort *	1 cup	250 ml
Butter, softened	1/4 cup	50 ml
Dark brown sugar, packed	1/4 cup	50 ml
Large eggs	2	2
Finely grated zest of 1 lemon		
Finely grated zest of 1 orange		
Sorghum flour	1/2 cup	125 ml
White rice flour	1/4 cup	50 ml
Coconut flour	1/4 cup	50 ml
Xanthan gum	1 tsp	5 ml
Baking soda	1/2 tsp	2 ml
Ground cinnamon	1 tsp	5 ml
Pecans, chopped	1/2 lb	250 g

A day or two before baking the cookies, chop dried fruits into pieces, mix in Southern Comfort, and cover.

Preheat oven to 325 F (165 C). Line baking sheets with parchment paper, or coat well with baking spray. Strain dried fruit mixture, leaving it in your sieve to drain while you prepare the rest of the cookie batter.

Cream butter and sugar until light and fluffy. Add eggs and zests, continue beating until eggs are fully incorporated and mixture is once again smooth and fluffy. In a separate bowl, combine flours, xanthan gum, baking soda, and cinnamon. Add most of it (reserve about 1/4 cup) to the butter & sugar mixture, beat gently until well combined. Add strained fruit to the reserved flour mixture, toss well to coat the pieces (to separate them a bit). Add coated fruit and pecans to the cookie batter, mix well.

Use a tablespoon, cookie scoop, or small ice cream scoop to drop rounded spoonfuls of the batter onto prepared baking sheets. Bake for 15-20 minutes, until golden brown. Allow to cool on sheets for 5 minutes or so, before gently transferring to baking racks to finish cooling. Once cookies are cool, keep them stored in airtight containers. Much like actual fruitcake, these tend to get even better with age!

* Southern Comfort is my favourite spirit to use in making fruitcake, but be aware: Southern Comfort is made from Bourbon, a spirit that is often distilled from (among other things) fermented wheat. While it doesn't cause a reaction in MOST people with gluten sensitivities - and the leading Celiac associations have deemed it gluten-free as of publication of this book - a few experts disagree. If you have noticed a reaction, or just want to play it extra safe, it could be a good idea forgo the Southern Comfort in favour of rum or brandy.

If you're looking to do an alcohol free version, simmer the dried fruit in fruit in juice or non-alcoholic wine it just until the fruit softens up and soaks up most of the liquid.

Gluten Free Fruitcake Cookies

Boozy Chocolate Haystack Cookies

Here's another childhood favorite that I saw fit to mess with. While the original was great, the addition of cream liqueur takes it to a whole new level. These are particularly fabulous with the "Baja" line of cream tequila liqueurs. I love it with Baja Rosa (Strawberry) and Baja Luna (Black Raspberry), but try it with any cream liqueur - Irish cream, Castries peanut creme, Godiva...yum! These are easy, fast, no-bake.. and OH so addictive!

Oats	3 cups	750 ml
Coconut	1 cup	250 ml
Sugar	2 cups	500 ml
Cream liqueur of choice	½ cup	125 ml
Butter	½ cup	125 ml
Cocoa	½ cup	125 ml

In a large bowl, combine oats and coconut, set aside. Prepare 2 cookie sheets - or a counter top - with parchment or waxed paper.

Combine sugar, liqueur, butter, and cocoa together in a medium saucepan. Heat to a boil, stirring constantly. Allow to boil for 2 minutes, remove from heat.

Pour hot mixture over coconut and oats, stir to coat everything evenly. Drop by rounded tablespoon onto prepared pans or counter top, allow to cool fully - cookies will harden and "set up" as they cool. Store in an airtight container - these will keep a long time, assuming they go uneaten that long!

Makes at least 24 cookies

Boozy Chocolate Haystack Cookies

Nanaimo Bars

Nanaimo Bars are an addictive, incredibly rich Canadian bar. It's a three layered bar that can be made in almost any flavor you can imagine. Flavor the buttercream layer with liqueur, or with homemade flavor extracts. Your imagination is your only limit!

Bottom Layer

Graham cracker crumbs	1 1/4 cups	300 ml
Finely chopped almonds	½ cup	125 ml
Coconut	1 cup	250 ml
Butter, melted	½ cup	125 ml
Sugar	1/4 cup	50 ml
Cocoa	1/3 cup	75 ml
Large egg, beaten	1	1

In a large bowl, combine graham crumbs, almonds, and coconut, set aside.

Combine butter, sugar, and cocoa in a small saucepan. Stir in beaten egg, mixing until fully incorporated. Cook mixture over low-medium heat, stirring constantly until thickened. Remove from heat. Pour hot mixture over crumbs mixture, stir to coat everything evenly. Dump mixture into an ungreased 8" x 8" pan, pressing firmly and evenly to form bottom layer across the bottom of the pan only.

Middle Layer

Butter	1 cup	250 ml
Liqueur of choice	1/3 cup	75 ml
Vanilla custard powder*	1/4 cup	50 ml
Powdered Sugar	4-5 cups	1000-1250 ml

Cream together butter, liqueur, and custard powder until well combined. Slowly add powdered sugar, a bit at a time, until mixture is very thick. Spread over bottom later, smoothing top as much as possible.

* Custard powder can be found in the import aisle of many grocery / specialty stores. Alternatively, use cook-and-serve pudding powder - NOT instant.

Top Layer

Baking chocolate squares	6 x 1oz	6 x 30 g
Butter	3 Tbsp	45 ml

In a small saucepan, melt butter and chocolate together over low heat. Remove from heat, allow to cool slightly. Once chocolate is cool - but still liquid - spread evenly over the middle layer. Chill bars in fridge for at least 30 minutes, or until chocolate topping has set. Cut into bars - about 1" x 2" is plenty big, these are extremely rich and sweet - a little goes a long way !

Flavor ideas:
While cream liqueur is amazing in this recipe, feel free to use it as a way to showcase your homemade flavor extracts as well. To do this, use 1/3 cup (75 ml) heavy cream in place of the liqueur, and add 1-3 tsp (5-15 ml) extract - start with 1 tsp, flavor to your taste!

Creme de Menthe Nanaimo Bars

Boozy Brownies

Chocolate of choice	8 oz	250 g
Butter	1 cup	250 ml
Large eggs	5	5
Brown sugar	1 ½ cups	375 ml
Sugar	1 ½ cups	375 ml
Liqueur of choice	½ cup	125 ml
Flour	1 ½ cups	375 ml

Preheat oven to 350°F (180°C) degrees. Prepare a 9 x 13" baking pan with cooking spray, or line with parchment paper. Chop chocolate into small chunks.

In a small saucepan, melt chocolate and butter together over low heat. Remove from heat, allow to cool slightly.

In a large mixing bowl, combine eggs, sugars, and liqueur until smooth. Stir in chocolate mixture, mixing until fully incorporated. Carefully add in flour, stirring until completely incorporated and smooth. Spread into prepared baking pan.

Bake for 35-40 minutes, or until knife or toothpick inserted into the center comes out mostly clean. Do not over bake! Cool to room temperature before cutting into bars. Makes 18 servings

Brownie flavor ideas:

Beer & Chocolate Brownies: Use dark chocolate, along with a stout. Guinness works well!

White Chocolate Martini "Brownies": Use white chocolate, along with Godiva liqueur

Buttery Nipple "Brownies": Use white chocolate, along with 1/4 cup each Butterscotch schnapps and Irish cream.

Toasted Almond Brownies: Use white or milk chocolate, along with 1/4 cup each Kahlua and amaretto

Boozy Brownies

Rum Raisin Tarts

Like Nanaimo bars, this recipe is based on a Canadian favorite - butter tarts. So very good!

Tart shells

Flour	1 1/4 cups	300 ml
Salt	½ tsp	2 ml
Sugar	2 Tbsp	30 ml
Butter, chilled	½ cup	125 ml
Ice cold water	1/4 cup	50 ml
Raisins	½ - 1 cup	125-250 ml

Filling

Large eggs	3	3
Butter, softened	1/3 cup	75 ml
Brown sugar	1 cup	250 ml
Rum	1/4 cup	50 ml

Combine flour, salt, and sugar together in a food processor. Cut butter into small cubes, add to mix, and process just until butter is broken up and incorporated, about 15-20 seconds. With the processor running, stream about half of the water into the flour mixture, just until dough starts to come together. If necessary, add more water, up to the full 1/4 cup. Remove dough from processor, gather into a ball. Flatten slightly, wrap tightly in plastic wrap, and chill for an hour.

Once dough has chilled, unwrap and transfer to a lightly floured work surface. Roll fairly thin - about 1/8", and cut into 4" rounds. Gently press into a lightly sprayed muffin pan - you can press the sides/bottom down to conform to the pan, or go fancy and leave the top edges fairly ruffled. Up to you! Divide raisins among prepared tart shells. Chill while making the filling.

Preheat oven to 375°F (190°C).

In a heavy, medium sized saucepan, whisk the eggs. Add butter, brown sugar, and rum, stirring until everything is fully incorporated into the mix. Cook over medium - low heat, stirring constantly. Bring just to a boil, and immediately remove from heat. Spoon filling into unbaked tart shells. Bake for 15-20 minutes or until filling has set and crusts are golden brown. Remove from oven, allow to cool to room temperature before removing tarts. Serve at room temperature.

Makes around 12 tarts.

Rum Raisin Tarts

Rum Raisin Bars

Crust

Butter	½ cup	125 ml
Powdered sugar	1/4 cup	50 ml
Flour	1 ½ cups	375 ml

Topping

Raisins	2 cups	500 ml
Rum	1/3 cup	75 ml
Butter, melted	3/4 cup	175 ml
Brown sugar	2 cups	500 ml
Large eggs, beaten	4	4

The night before baking, place raisins in a glass bowl, separating any clumps of raisins that stick together. Add rum, stir slightly, cover and allow to soak overnight. The next day, preheat oven to 350°F (180°C). Prepare a 9 x 13" baking pan with nonstick spray.

Crust: Melt butter in a medium saucepan. Add powdered sugar and flour, stirring until fully incorporated and smooth. Remove from heat, press evenly into bottom of prepared baking pan. Bake for 5 minutes.

Topping: Combine butter and brown sugar in a medium saucepan, stir until smooth. Add eggs, beat until fully incorporated and smooth. Cook over low heat until mixture just reaches a low simmer. Remove from heat, stir in raisins and any rum that did not get absorbed by them. Spoon mixture over baked crust. Return bars to oven, bake for 25-30 minutes or until topping is set. Cool to room temperature before cutting and serving. Best served chilled!

Bananas Foster Pralines

A New Orleans favorite, with a twist! Well, two New Orleans favorites, really. Two twists? A double helix of New Orleans favorites? Whatever the description... these are very tasty!

Sugar	1 ½ cups	375 ml
Brown sugar, packed	3/4 cup	175 ml
Rum	1/4 cup	50 ml
Heavy cream	1/4 cup	50 ml
Creme de banane	2 Tbsp	30 ml
Cinnamon	½ tsp	2 ml
Butter	2/3 cup	150 ml
Pecans, chopped	3/4 cup	175 ml
Dried banana slices, chopped	3/4 cup	175 ml

Line baking sheets with parchment paper, set aside.

In a heavy, medium sized saucepan, combine sugars, rum, heavy cream, creme de banane, cinnamon, and butter. Mixture will be VERY thick! Cook, over medium-high heat until mixture comes to a boil, reduce heat to medium-low heat. Affix a candy thermometer to the side of the pan. Cook at a low boil, stirring occasionally, until mixture reaches 239°F (115°C)

Remove from heat. Add the pecans and banana chips, stirring until the mixture begins to thicken and becomes creamy and cloudy. Working quickly, spoon onto prepared baking sheets. Allow to cool completely before serving. Pralines can be wrapped in plastic wrap and/or stored in an airtight container.

Margarita Macadamia Brittle

After my Jalapeno Beer Brittle (next!) turned out to be such a hit, I had to experiment with other unique boozy brittle ideas. Of course :)

Sugar	1 cup	250 ml
Light corn syrup	½ cup	125 ml
Salt	1/4 tsp	1 ml
Tequila	1/3 cup	75 ml
Zest and juice of 2 limes		
Baking soda	1 tsp	5 ml
Butter	2 Tbsp	30 ml
Macadamia nuts, chopped	1 ½ cups	375 ml
Cooking spray		

Set oven to "warm", or lowest temperature. Spray a large cookie sheet with cooking spray, place inside warm oven.

Combine sugar, corn syrup, salt, tequila, and lime zest / juice in a large, heavy saucepan. Bring to boil over medium-high heat, then attach candy thermometer to saucepan. Stir often until temperature reaches 300°F (150°C). Keep a very close eye on it - after about 280°F (138°C), as the temperature has a tendency to race up at that point. If you turn your back, you could burn it!

At 300°F (150°C), remove the pan from heat, add baking soda and butter, stir until incorporated. Quickly add in macadamia nuts and stir until completely coated.

Remove cookie sheet from oven, and pour brittle out onto it. Working quickly, use two buttered forks to pull the brittle mixture out from the center, until it is thinly spread and relatively even. Cool completely, then break into pieces.

Jalapeno Beer Brittle

I'd been promising my husband a beer-based brittle for a very long time. When I finally got around to fulfilling that promise, I decided to get funky with it - coming up with this recipe for his new treat! Using roasted, salted peanuts along with a dark, flavorful beer and jalapenos makes this a very "guy friendly" snack.

The way the jalapenos cook in the syrup gives the brittle an even, "low, slow burn", not so in-your-face with the jalapeno kick. Very tasty, even though I can't stand beer!

Jalapeno peppers	1-3	1-3
Sugar	1 cup	250 ml
Light corn syrup	½ cup	125 ml
Salt	1/4 tsp	1 ml
Beer of choice	1/3 cup	75 ml
Baking soda	1 tsp	5 ml
Butter	2 Tbsp	30 ml
Roasted salted peanuts	1 ½ cups	375 ml
Cooking spray		

Set oven to "warm", or lowest temperature. Spray a large cookie sheet with cooking spray, place inside warm oven.

Finely chop jalapeno peppers. Remove seeds and rib meat if you prefer - leaving them in adds heat. Combine sugar, corn syrup, salt, beer, and jalapeno pepper bits in a large, heavy saucepan. Bring to boil over medium-high heat, then attach candy thermometer to saucepan. Stir often until temperature reaches 300°F (150°C). Keep a very close eye on it - after about 280°F (138°C), as the temperature has a tendency to race up at that point. If you turn your back, you could burn it!

At 300°F (150°C), remove the pan from heat, add baking soda and butter, stir until incorporated. Quickly add in peanuts and stir until completely coated. Remove cookie sheet from oven, and pour brittle out onto it. Working quickly, use two buttered forks to pull the brittle mixture out from the center, until it is thinly spread and relatively even. Cool completely, then break into pieces.

Jalapeno Beer Brittle

Hop Flavored Beer Lollipops - LolliHOPS!

Around the same time I created the hop flavored dark chocolate truffles in the "Fancy" chapter, I also created this recipe for my husband, who LOVES his hops. Amazingly enough, I even find these to be quite tasty, and I don't even like beer!

Small amount of butter		
Beer of choice (We used an IPA)	½ cup	125 ml
Dried hop cones (we used Centennial)*	6	6
Sugar	1 cup	250 ml
Light corn syrup	½ cup	125 ml
Lollipop sticks		

Use butter to generously grease the back of 1 or 2 baking sheets, set aside.

Heat beer to a light simmer. Break up hop cones into leaves, add to warm beer. Remove from heat, allow to simmer for about 10 minutes.

Strain beer into a measuring glass, measuring only 1/3 cup. (The 1/2 cup measurement is to allow for some evaporation / hop leaf absorption). In a heavy saucepan (2 quart), mix together sugar, corn syrup, and strained 1/3 cup of beer.

Bring to boil over medium-high heat, then attach candy thermometer to saucepan. Stir often until temperature reaches 300 degrees F (150 degrees Celcius). KEEP A VERY CLOSE EYE ON IT after about 280 degrees, as the temp has a tendency to race up at that point. If you turn your back, you could burn it!

At 300 degrees, remove the pan from heat. Allow to cool & thicken slightly, stirring constantly – about 1 minute.

Working quickly, drop small amounts of the hot sugar mixture onto the greased baking sheets – about 1-3 tsp(s) per, depending on the desired size of your lollihops. Lay a lollipop stick into each circle, so that the tip is near the center of the lollipop, and flat against the surface. (ie, you want it parallel to the baking sheet, not perpendicular to it!). Carefully give each stick a bit of a twirl, so that the candy coats around the stick to hold it in place.

Cool completely, carefully remove from baking sheets. Wrap with plastic, waxed paper, parchment paper, or whatever. Enjoy!

* Hops can vary wildly in size and flavor. Be sure to taste as you go – you may not want to use the whole 10 minute steeping time. If you don't have access to whole dried hope cones, you can use 1/4 tsp – 1/2 tsp of hop pellets! It doesn't take much, so your next batch of homebrew won't miss it!

Lollihops

Basic Boozy Ice Cream

"Boozy" may be a bit of a misnomer in this recipe, and in all of the ice cream recipes that follow. When making ice cream - even more so than any of the other recipes in this book - much of the alcohol is cooked off in the process. In the case of ice cream, it's vitally important to cook off most of the alcohol! With too much alcohol in the mix, the ice cream will not freeze properly. This recipe produces a full bodied, very rich, flavorful ice cream.

Cream liqueur of choice*	1 cup	250 ml
Large egg yolks	8	8
Sugar	3/4 cup	175 ml
Whole milk	1 cup	250 ml
Heavy cream	2 ½ cups	625 ml
Salt	1/4 tsp	1 ml

Measure cream liqueur into a medium sized saucepan. Bring to a boil over medium heat, then reduce temperature to low or medium-low, just hot enough to keep the liqueur at a light simmer. Simmer for 10-15 minutes, or until reduced to half its original volume.

Combine egg yolks and sugar in a medium mixing bowl. Whisk for a few minutes, until fluffy, pale yellow, and smooth. Add whole milk, whisk until well incorporated.

Add heavy cream and salt to hot liqueur, stir until well combined. Stream egg mixture into saucepan, whisking to incorporate. Cook over medium heat, stirring constantly, until mixture thickens - it should be thick enough to coat the back of a spoon. Remove from heat, cool to room temperature, and then chill thoroughly until ready to use.

Follow your ice cream maker's instructions to freeze custard mixture. Serve immediately for a soft ice cream, or freeze for at least 2 hours for a more firm ice cream. Keep any extra ice cream solution chilled until use - process into ice cream within a day or two. Makes about 1 ½ quarts.

* Non-cream based liqueur can also be used. If using a non-cream liqueur, use 3/4 cup (175 ml) liqueur, and increase heavy cream to 2 3/4 cups (675 ml)

Tiramisu Ice Cream

Kahlua	½ cup	125 ml
Large egg yolks	6	6
Sugar	3/4 cup	175 ml
Mascarpone cheese, softened	1 cup	250 ml
Whole milk	1 cup	250 ml
Heavy cream	1 ½ cups	375 ml
Salt	1/4 tsp	1 ml

Measure Kahlua into a medium sized saucepan. Bring to a boil over medium heat, then reduce temperature to low or medium-low, just hot enough to keep the liqueur at a light simmer. Simmer for 10-15 minutes, or until reduced to half its original volume.

Combine egg yolks and sugar in a medium mixing bowl. Whisk for a few minutes, until fluffy, pale yellow, and smooth. Add mascarpone cheese and whole milk, whisk until well incorporated and smooth.

Add heavy cream and salt to hot liqueur, stir until well combined. Stream egg mixture into saucepan, whisking to incorporate. Cook over medium heat, stirring constantly, until mixture thickens - it should be thick enough to coat the back of a spoon. Remove from heat, cool to room temperature, and then chill thoroughly until ready to use.

Follow your ice cream maker's instructions to freeze custard mixture. Serve immediately for a soft ice cream, or freeze for at least 2 hours for a more firm ice cream. Keep any extra ice cream solution chilled until use - process into ice cream within a day or two.

To serve, dust with cocoa powder and garnish with lady finger cookies, if desired. Makes about 1 ½ quarts.

Mint Julep Ice Cream

Bourbon		1 cup		250 ml
Mint leaves		1 cup		250 ml
Heavy cream		3 cups		750 ml
Whole milk		1 cup		250 ml
Large egg yolks	6		6	
Sugar		1 cup		250 ml
Salt		1 tsp		5 ml

Measure bourbon into a medium sized saucepan. Bring to a boil over medium heat, then reduce temperature to low or medium-low, just hot enough to keep the liqueur at a light simmer. Simmer for 10-15 minutes, or until reduced to about half its original volume.

Once bourbon has reduced in volume, remove from heat. Muddle mint leaves with heavy cream, add to hot bourbon. Return to heat, bring just to a boil. Remove from heat and allow to steep for 10-15 minutes. Remove mint from cream mixture, squeezing liquid from the leaves. Discard the leaves.

In a separate bowl, beat egg yolks together with sugar and salt. When thoroughly combined, add whole milk and whisk till smooth. Allow milk mixture to cool slightly, then add in egg mixture, whisking till fully combined and smooth. Heat just to the boiling point, stirring constantly. Remove from heat, cool to room temperature, and then chill thoroughly until ready to use.

Follow your ice cream maker's instructions to freeze custard mixture. Serve immediately for a soft ice cream, or freeze for at least 2 hours for a more firm ice cream. Keep any extra ice cream solution chilled until use - process into ice cream within a day or two. Makes about 2 quarts

Mango Mojito Ice Cream

Rum	1 ½ cups	375 ml
Mint leaves	1 cup	250 ml
Heavy cream	3 cups	750 ml
Large egg yolks	6	6
Sugar	3/4 cup	175 ml
Salt	1 tsp	5 ml
Canned mango pulp	1 ½ cups	375 ml

Measure rum into a medium sized saucepan. Bring to a boil over medium heat, then reduce temperature to low or medium-low, just hot enough to keep the liqueur at a light simmer. Simmer for 10-15 minutes, or until reduced to about half its original volume.

Once rum has reduced in volume, remove from heat. Muddle mint leaves with heavy cream, add to hot rum. Return to heat, bring just to a boil. Remove from heat and allow to steep for 10-15 minutes. Remove mint from cream mixture, squeezing liquid from the leaves. Discard the leaves.

In a separate bowl, beat egg yolks together with sugar and salt. When thoroughly combined, add mango pulp and whisk till smooth. Allow milk mixture to cool slightly, then add in mango mixture, whisking till fully combined and smooth. Heat just to the boiling point, stirring constantly. Remove from heat, cool to room temperature, and then chill thoroughly until ready to use.

Follow your ice cream maker's instructions to freeze custard mixture. Serve immediately for a soft ice cream, or freeze for at least 2 hours for a more firm ice cream. Keep any extra ice cream solution chilled until use - process into ice cream within a day or two. Makes about 2 quarts

Mango Mojito Ice Cream

Pina Colada Ice Cream

Rum	1 cup	250 ml
Large egg yolks	6	6
Sugar	3/4 cup	175 ml
Pina colada mix	1 cup	250 ml
Heavy cream	2½ cups	625 ml
Salt	1/4 tsp	1 ml
Coconut	1 cup	250 ml
Crushed pineapple, drained	1 cup	250 ml

Measure rum into a medium sized saucepan. Bring to a boil over medium heat, then reduce temperature to low or medium-low, just hot enough to keep the liqueur at a light simmer. Simmer for 10-15 minutes, or until reduced to half its original volume.

Combine egg yolks and sugar in a medium mixing bowl. Whisk for a few minutes, until fluffy, pale yellow, and smooth. Add pina colada mix, whisk until well incorporated and smooth.

Add heavy cream and salt to hot liqueur, stir until well combined. Stream egg mixture into saucepan, whisking to incorporate. Cook over medium heat, stirring constantly, until mixture thickens - it should be thick enough to coat the back of a spoon. Remove from heat, cool to room temperature, and then chill thoroughly until ready to use.

Follow your ice cream maker's instructions to freeze custard mixture. Remove ice cream from ice cream maker, stir in coconut and crushed pineapple.

Serve immediately for a soft ice cream, or freeze for at least 2 hours for a more firm ice cream. Keep any extra ice cream solution chilled until use - process into ice cream within a day or two. Makes about 2 quarts.

Basic Boozy Sorbet

A sorbet is a frozen dessert made from fruit juices, fruit pulp, etc.. but not containing eggs or dairy products. For that reason, you'll need to stick to non-cream based liqueurs for this set of recipes. Sorbet is popular as a "diet friendly" dessert, as it doesn't have any of the fat found in ice cream. Depending on the area, this is also sometimes referred to as sherbet, Italian ice, etc.

Much like the ice cream, the final product here won't technically be "boozy" - cooking off a large amount of the alcohol is important to actually being able to freeze the stuff. You know. Being a frozen dessert and all!

This is a base recipe, a good starting point. Sugar can be adjusted, based on whatever fruit you use. Use juice or water, just play with it!

Liqueur of choice	½ cup	125 ml
Water or juice	½ cup	125 ml
Sugar	1 ½ cups	375 ml
Fresh lemon juice	1/4 cup	50 ml
Fruit Puree*	3 cups	750 ml

Measure liqueur into a medium sized saucepan. Bring to a boil over medium heat, then reduce temperature to low or medium-low, just hot enough to keep the liqueur at a light simmer. Simmer for 10-15 minutes, or until reduced to half its original volume.

Add water or juice, sugar, and lemon juice., heating to a simmer. Stir until all of the sugar is dissolved. Add in fruit puree or juice, stirring well. Bring to a boil, then remove from heat.

Allow sorbet to cool to room temperature, strain if desired, then transfer to fridge to chill thoroughly. Follow your ice cream maker's instructions to freeze fruit mixture.

Serve immediately for a soft sorbet, or freeze for at least 1 hours for a more firm sorbet. Keep any extra fruit mixture chilled until use - process into frozen sorbet within a day or two. Makes about 2 quarts.

* Juice can be used instead of puree, if desired. This especially makes sense for fruits like lemons, limes, oranges, grapefruits, and pomegranates.

Flavor combination ideas:

Apple: Use 3 cups (750 ml) apple cider in place of fruit puree, decrease sugar to 1 1/4 cups (300 ml). Flavor with apple brandy.

Blueberry: Fresh, pureed blueberries with amaretto!

Citrus: Use juice(s) of fresh lemons, limes, oranges, and/or grapefruit, along with a little fresh zest. Use Triple sec or Grand Marnier for the liqueur. Try lime juice and rum for a "daiquiri" sorbet! Lemon juice, a little triple sec, and Jack Daniel's for the liqueur makes a "Lynchburg Lemonade" sorbet.

Mango: Use fresh or canned mango puree - make sure the fruit is very ripe if you are using fresh. Decrease sugar to 1 1/4 cups (300 ml). This is particularly great with rum, but try Grand Marnier, POM liqueur, or Limoncello.

Peaches: Pureed peaches (use the water, or lemon juice to aid in pureeing!) go especially great with amaretto or Southern Comfort. Cook peaches a little longer, and puree again after cooking for an extra smooth texture.

Strawberries: Use pureed fresh strawberries with orange juice instead of water, and Grand Marnier for the liqueur. Works well with Blackberries, blueberries, and raspberries as well.

Another idea if to use lime juice in place of the lemon juice, and rum for the liqueur - strawberry daiquiri sorbet! Alternatively, use tequila instead of rum for a strawberry margarita sorbet.

Fruity

Fruit and liqueurs go so well together, they really needed their own chapter. Sure, the rest of this book is littered with other fruity recipes... but this section is for all of the yummy fruit based recipes that simply didn't fit elsewhere. I'm starting this off with a bang - Pavlovas. I could LIVE on Pavlovas - no joke. Not only are they my favorite dessert ever - EVER! - they're one of my top 3 favorite foods in general. Yes, a lifetime of Pavlovas, cheese, and sushi.. and I'd be one satisfied woman!

Don't let the length of the Pavlova recipe section scare you. It's mostly me babbling. That's just what Pavlova does to me! Pavlovas are actually quite easy to make, and take very little in the way of ingredients.

Pavlova!

Yes, this is the only recipe in the book with an exclamation point in its title. Pavlovas are my absolute favorite dessert of all time! They're basically a type of large meringue - one which is crispy on the outside, and like a giant, fluffy marshmallow on the inside! - heaped with whipped cream, then topped with fruit. Does it get any better? No. No, it doesn't! I love exposing people to this dessert, I love watching their eyes pop when they bite in to a pav for the first time.

Nice light texture, and a wonderful way to enjoy fresh fruit. Perfect summer dessert for entertaining, and this is a really easy recipe for anyone. A quick head's up though - if your meringue is not cracked by the time you remove it from the oven, it will likely crack at some other point, and will almost certainly crack when you start garnishing. Don't worry! Totally normal, no one will notice or care!

Pavlovas are either an Australian dessert, or a New Zealand dessert, depending on who you ask. The two of them have a lot of national pride wrapped up in Pavlova wars, and in my mind, if there's something worth fighting over, it's Pavlova. Legend has it that a chef in one of the two countries was so enamored with Anna Pavlova - a famous ballerina in the early 20th century - that he created this dessert in her honor. Can you imagine having a man so in love with you, that he'd create perfection itself? Amazing. I digress. The fluffy meringue base and whipped cream are said to represent her tutus.

As with most/all recipes that require egg whites for structure, it is brutally important that the egg whites are completely free of ANY egg yolk bits. I'm not kidding - not even a speck. Even a tiny amount will prevent them from whipping up like they're supposed to. If you're not very confident in your egg-cracking prowess, try cracking them individually into a little bowl before transferring them to the mixer. If you get a bit of egg yolk in one, you can just chuck it without ruining the whole batch. Also, be sure that your mixer and whisk attachment are very clean, free from any grease at all.

Pavlova

Large egg whites	4	4
Super fine / castor sugar*	1 cup	250 ml
Salt	1/8 tsp	½ ml
Non-cream liqueur of choice**	3 Tbsp	45 ml
or		
Homemade flavor extract	2 tsp	10 ml
White vinegar	2 tsp	10 ml
Cornstarch	1 tsp	5 ml
Heavy cream	1 1/4 cup	300 ml
Non-cream liqueur of choice	2 Tbsp	30 ml
or		
Homemade flavor extract	1 tsp	5 ml
Sugar, optional	2 Tbsp	30 ml

Fresh Fruits & Berries

Preheat oven to 350°F (180°C). Remove eggs from fridge and allow to warm to room temp (about 5 minutes). Line a baking sheet with parchment paper, and set aside. Fit your electric mixer with the whisk attachment.

In your mixer bowl, beat egg whites together with salt until glossy peaks form. Slowly add in the sugar, and continue whipping until stiff peaks form. Turn off mixer, remove bowl. Sprinkle liqueur or extract**, vinegar, and cornstarch over meringue, gently fold in till combined.

Heap meringue onto the center of your baking sheet. Use a spatula to spread the meringue out to approximately an 8-9" circle. I like to have my meringue a fairly even depth throughout - some like a mound, some like it to be a little concave. If you want to get really fancy, put the meringue into a pastry bag and pipe it out as a mass of swirls that form your 8" circle! It's really up to you!

Put the baking sheet into your oven, and immediately turn the temperature down to 250°F (120°C). Bake for 1 hour and 20 minutes. Once your timer goes off, turn the oven off and let the meringue cool in the oven for several hours. The baking of the meringue can be done the day before, if needed.

Just before serving, whip the heavy cream. I like my Pavlovas a little sweeter, so I add about 2 Tbsp of sugar - add as much or as little as you want. Purists may not want to sweeten the cream at all! Mound the whipped cream on your Pavlova, and top with fresh fruits. Serve immediately!

Serves 4-6. (Or 2 Pavlova fanatics! Or one, if it's ME! Muaha!)

* Super fine / castor sugar is granulated sugar with a much finer grain size than regular granulated sugar. It is NOT powdered / icing sugar! Super fine sugar is usually sold near the sugar in the baking aisle, in small boxes - sometimes resembling milk cartons. If you aren't able to find actual super fine sugar, you can process regular granulated sugar in your food processor until fine. Measure AFTER you process.

** It is very important to not use a cream based liqueur to flavor the meringue itself. Any fat at all, whether from a cream based liqueur, or oil based flavoring. Fat added to the meringue will cause it to break down. Feel free to use cream or oil based flavorings in the whipped cream topping, however!

Pavlova Flavor ideas:

The possibilities for flavoring your Pavlova are endless! Use any non-cream based liqueur to flavor the meringue, or use it as a great venue for displaying your homemade flavor extracts from the first chapter. Use anything you want to flavor the cream, and top with any combination of fruits that strikes your fancy. It really is a truly versatile, amazing dessert.

Here are a few of my favorite combinations:

- Rum in the both the meringue and whipped cream. Top with sliced bananas, mango, and toasted coconut.

- Rum in the both the meringue and whipped cream. Marinate sliced mangos in rum overnight. Top whipped cream with a drizzle of mango puree, marinated mangos, a squeeze of lime juice, and thinly sliced fresh mint leaves.

- Grand Marnier in both the meringue and whipped cream. Top with sliced strawberries and kiwis, drizzle with 1 Tbsp grand marnier.

- POM Pomegranate liqueur in both meringue and whipped cream. Top with mango or mandarin orange sections (canned works best) and the flesh of 1-2 pomegranates.

- Amaretto in both the meringue and whipped cream. Top with strawberries, raspberries, and blueberries, garnishing with fresh mint leaves.

- Green tea extract in meringue and whipped cream. Top with thin slices of honeydew and cantaloupe.

- Substitute half of the sugar with light brown sugar. Use rum flavoring in the meringue & whipped cream. Top with cooled bananas foster and pecans!

Chocolate Pavlova

Same warnings about egg yolk and fat apply here, of course!

Large egg whites	4	4
Super fine / castor sugar*	1 cup	250 ml
Salt	1/8 tsp	½ ml
Cocoa	1/4 cup	50 ml
Non-cream liqueur of choice**	3 Tbsp	45 ml
or		
Homemade flavor extract	2 tsp	10 ml
White vinegar	2 tsp	10 ml
Cornstarch	1 tsp	5 ml
Heavy cream	1 1/4 cup	300 ml
Cocoa powder	2-3 Tbsp	30-45 ml
Non-cream liqueur of choice	2 Tbsp	30 ml
or		
Homemade flavor extract	1 tsp	5 ml
Sugar, optional	2 Tbsp	30 ml

Fresh Fruits & Berries

Preheat oven to 350°F (180°C). Remove eggs from fridge and allow to warm to room temp (about 5 minutes). Line a baking sheet with parchment paper, and set aside. Fit your electric mixer with the whisk attachment.

In your mixer bowl, beat egg whites together with salt until glossy peaks form. Slowly add in the sugar, and continue whipping until stiff peaks form. Turn speed down to lowest setting, sprinkle in cocoa powder, run mixer just until cocoa is incorporated. Turn off mixer, remove bowl. Sprinkle liqueur or extract**, vinegar, and cornstarch over meringue, gently fold in till combined.

Heap meringue onto the center of your baking sheet. Use a spatula to spread the meringue out to approximately an 8-9" circle. I like to have my meringue a fairly even depth throughout - some like a mound, some like it to be a little concave. If you want to get really fancy, put the meringue into a pastry bag and pipe it out as a mass of swirls that form your 8" circle! It's really up to you!

Put the baking sheet into your oven, and immediately turn the temperature down to 250°F (120°C). Bake for 1 hour and 20 minutes. Once your timer goes off, turn the oven off and let the meringue cool in the oven for several hours. The baking of the meringue can be done the day before, if needed.

Just before serving, whip the heavy cream with the cocoa and flavoring. I like my Pavlovas a little sweeter, so I add about 2 Tbsp of sugar - add as much or as little as you want. Purists may not want to sweeten the cream at all!

Mound the whipped cream on your Pavlova, and top with fresh fruits. Serve immediately!

Serves 4-6. (Or 2 Pavlova fanatics!)

* Super fine / castor sugar is granulated sugar with a much finer grain size than regular granulated sugar. It is NOT powdered / icing sugar! Super fine sugar is usually sold near the sugar in the baking aisle, in small boxes - sometimes resembling milk cartons. If you aren't able to find actual super fine sugar, you can process regular granulated sugar in your food processor until fine. Measure AFTER you process.

** It is very important to not use a cream based liqueur to flavor the meringue itself. Any fat at all, whether from a cream based liqueur, or oil based flavoring. Fat added to the meringue will cause it to break down. Feel free to use cream or oil based flavorings in the whipped cream topping, however!

Flavor and Serving ideas:

Use any non-cream based liqueur to flavor the meringue, or use it as a great venue for displaying your homemade flavor extracts from the first chapter. Use anything you want to flavor the cream, and top with any combination of fruits that strikes your fancy. It really is a truly versatile, amazing dessert.

With chocolate Pavlovas, feel free to play up the chocolate in your toppings. Drizzle with chocolate syrup, garnish with chocolate shavings... whatever you want!

Here are a few of my favorite combinations:

- Chambord in the meringue and whipped cream, top with chocolate sauce and raspberries. For an added kick, marinate the raspberries in a little Chambord before use.

- Creme de Cacao in the meringue, Irish cream in the whipped cream, topped with sliced strawberries.

- Grand Marnier in the meringue, Kahlua in the whipped cream, topped with canned (drained) mandarin orange sections and drizzled with chocolate sauce.

- Rum in the meringue and whipped cream, topped with sliced bananas and chocolate sauce

Fruit Flambé

Flambés? I have no idea if that's pluralizable. Whatever! Flambéd fruit is fruit that has been cooked in a boozy sauce on a stove top, then lit on fire. How awesome is that? It makes an impressive display for dinner guests, and is a relatively safe way to indulge your inner pyromaniac. Heh. Fire!

Now by "relatively", I mean that yes, there is some risk. You have to take some precautions, and pay attention to what you're doing. If you manage to mess up and burn your house down, I'm not assuming liability for that. Just wanted to get that out of the way.

For each of these recipes, follow the recipe. Don't add more alcohol, or a higher proof alcohol, or try to get crazy with it in any other way. Just do it. Be sure to remove your pan from the burner before adding the alcohol, and use a long stick match or grill lighter to light the thing ablaze. Don't be peering over the edge of the pan when you light it, and if you're wearing a ton of hair spray... maybe have someone else do the honors. Either way, proceed at your own risk!

Now that I've got you good and scared... Flambéd fruit is not only a great display, it tastes amazing. Hot fruit with a bit of the taste of the alcohols used, caramelized in brown sugar... so good. Serve any of these as a sauce over vanilla ice cream, bake into a pie or tart, or serve on their own. Give it a go, just be careful!

Caramelized Brandied Pears

These are especially good with 1/4 tsp cardamom added in!

Butter, softened	1/4 cup	50 ml
Dark brown sugar, packed	½ cup	125 ml
Pear juice or nectar	½ cup	125 ml
Ripe pears, sliced *	4	4
Brandy	1/3 cup	75 ml

Combine butter, brown sugar, and pear juice together in a large skillet or frying pan. Cook over medium heat until butter is melted, and sauce is smooth. Add pear slices to the pan, continuing to cook until softened and beginning to caramelize. Remove from heat.

Carefully add brandy to the pan, swirling it slightly. Use a long handled match or BBQ lighter to ignite the rum. Once the flames die down, serve immediately, spooning the sauce over the fruit slices.

* Pears can be halved - remove the core, quartered, or sliced thickly.

Bananas Foster

This was my first foray into the world of fruit pyromania, and is still a favorite! You can leave out the cinnamon and creme de banane for a basic banane flambé .. Or omit the cinnamon and creme de banane, swapping the rum for Ouzo or Sambuca for a more adventurous dessert!

Butter, softened	1/4 cup	50 ml
Dark brown sugar, packed	½ cup	125 ml
Cinnamon	½ tsp	125 ml
Creme de banane liqueur	1/3 cup	75 ml
Bananas, peeled and sliced*	4	4
Dark rum	1/3 cup	75 ml

Combine butter, brown sugar, cinnamon , and creme de banane liqueur together in a large skillet or frying pan. Cook over medium heat until butter is melted, and sauce is smooth. Add banana slices to the pan, continuing to cook until softened. Remove from heat.

Carefully add rum to the pan, swirling it slightly. Use a long handled match or BBQ lighter to ignite the rum. Once the flames die down, serve immediately, spooning the sauce over the fruit slices.

* Traditionally, Bananas Foster is served as long wedges or slices of banana. I personally prefer to slice the bananas as longish diagonally cut disks, and others prefer just regular slices. Go with whatever you prefer!

Whisky Peaches

This recipe is also great with rum, rather than whisky. My personal favorite, however, is to use Southern Comfort with chopped pecans!

Butter, softened	1/4 cup	50 ml
Dark brown sugar, packed	½ cup	125 ml
Peach nectar or Grand Marnier	½ cup	125 ml
Ripe peaches, sliced or halved	4	4
Whisky	1/3 cup	75 ml

Combine butter, brown sugar, and peach nectar together in a large skillet or frying pan. Cook over medium heat until butter is melted, and sauce is smooth. Add peach slices to the pan, continuing to cook until softened and beginning to caramelize. Remove from heat. Carefully add whisky to the pan, swirling it slightly. Use a long handled match or BBQ lighter to ignite the rum. Once the flames die down, serve immediately, spooning the sauce over the fruit slices.

Brandied Apples

This recipe is what Christmas tastes like. New Year's Eve, too. Very "Winter Holiday"-ish. Yum!

Butter, softened	1/4 cup	50 ml
Dark brown sugar, packed	½ cup	125 ml
Cinnamon	1 tsp	5 ml
Nutmeg	½ tsp	2 ml
Apple cider	½ cup	125 ml
Apples, sliced *	3	3
Brandy	1/3 cup	75 ml

Combine butter, brown sugar, cinnamon, nutmeg, and apple cider together in a large skillet or frying pan. Cook over medium heat until butter is melted, and sauce is smooth. Add apple slices to the pan, continuing to cook until softened and beginning to caramelize. Remove from heat.

Carefully add brandy to the pan, swirling it slightly. Use a long handled match or BBQ lighter to ignite the rum. Once the flames die down, serve immediately, spooning the sauce over the fruit slices.

* Apples should be cored and thickly sliced.

Mangos Diablo

Like a mango margarita, in dessert form. Try a sprinkling of sea salt when served, to evoke the margarita madness! This also works well with pineapple slices.

Butter, softened	1/4 cup	50 ml
Dark brown sugar, packed	3/4 cup	175 ml
Grand Marnier	1 Tbsp	15 ml
Fresh squeezed lime juice	2 Tbsp	30 ml
Ripe mangos, prepared *	3	3
Tequila	1/3 cup	75 ml

Combine butter, brown sugar, Grand Marnier and lime juice together in a large skillet or frying pan. Cook over medium heat until butter is melted, and sauce is smooth. Add mango slices to the pan, continuing to cook until softened and beginning to caramelize. Remove from heat.
Carefully add brandy to the pan, swirling it slightly. Use a long handled match or BBQ lighter to ignite the rum. Once the flames die down, serve immediately, spooning the sauce over the fruit slices.

* Mangos should be peeled, pitted, and thickly sliced

Cherries Jubilee

Sugar	1/3 cup	75 ml
Corn starch	2 Tbsp	30 ml
Fresh orange juice	1/4 cup	50 ml
Fresh Lemon juice	2 Tbsp	30 ml
Freshly grated orange zest	2 tsp	10 ml
Dark, sweet ripe cherries, pitted	1 lb	500 g
Brandy	1/3 cup	75 ml

Combine sugar, corn starch, and juices together in a large skillet or frying pan, whisking until smooth. Cook over medium heat, continuing to whisk until sauce thickens.

Add orange zest and cherries to the pan, stirring to combine well. Bring to a boil, then reduce heat to low and simmer for 10 minutes. Remove from heat.

Carefully add brandy to the pan, swirling it slightly. Use a long handled match or BBQ lighter to ignite the rum. Once the flames die down, serve immediately, spooning the sauce over the fruit slices.

Poached Fruit

Here's another recipe that's going to take a large amount of space to deal with, when it's actually wickedly simple. Tons of options, that's all!

Poached fruit is a great way to use fruit when it's either off-season and less than perfect, or just a bit under ripe. The fruit is cooked in a flavorful liquid - usually wine - that is sweetened with sugar and/or honey, and flavored with any number of ingredients.

This cooking process sweetens and softens the fruit, so you're actually quite a bit better off starting with firm and under-ripe! Stone fruit - peaches, nectarines, apricots, plums, etc - are great to work with, but apples and pears (Bosc works best!) are also popular choices. The key is to go with a firm fruit that won't just turn to mush when poached.

Along with the base recipe, you'll find many flavor combinations to try - or just run wild with your own imagination! Poached fruit is great when served as slices on top of cheesecakes (or other desserts), on ice cream... served in halves or as whole fruit. A whole poached pear, perched in a martini glass and drizzled with a little chocolate is a statement kind of dessert!

Let's look at a gorgeous photo of sangria poached pears, before getting to the recipe. Ah, the joys of formatting a cookbook....!

Pears Poached in Sangria

179

Large fruit of choice	4	4
Liquid of choice *	3 cups	750 ml
Sugar	3/4 - 1 cup	175-250 ml
Flavoring items of choice *		

Prepare the fruit. All fruit should be peeled. For most stone fruits, it helps to boil the fruit for a couple of minutes, then run under cold water. This helps loosen the skin, and will enable it to peel off easily. After removing skin, remove pit or core, and slice the fruit thickly, if desired.

In a medium saucepan, combine your liquid(s) of choice with sugar, bring to a boil. Cook, stirring until all sugar is dissolved. Turn the heat down to low, add flavoring items of choice. At this point, it's a good idea to taste the syrup to make sure that the liquid is sweet enough for your taste. Add the fruit to the pot. If the fruit floats, laying a small, heat proof dish on top of it to weigh it down works well. Cover the pot and allow the fruit to cook through to desired softness - this may happen in 10 minutes, it may take 40-60 minutes. Just poke it every once in awhile to see how it's doing.

Once fruit is cooked through, remove from heat and allow to cool to room temperature. Once cool, move to fridge to chill for at least an hour. When ready to serve, remove fruit from poaching liquid. To make a sauce to serve with the fruit, return the poaching liquid to the stove top, simmer until reduced in volume and thickened.

* Liquid choices: Wine - red, white, rose, champagne, mead - any type that you like drinking. Favorite spirits, such as rum, whisky, and brandy can also be used. Fruit juice or water can be added for extra flavor, or to cut too-strong flavors.

* Flavoring items of choice: Vanilla beans (cut in half, lengthwise), whole cloves, zest/juice of citrus fruits, tea bags, cinnamon sticks, mint leaves, rosemary... whatever you feel like using! I recommend not using too many different flavors - I like to let the flavor of the fruit shine through.

Flavor Ideas:

- Peaches poached in 1 cup (250 ml) each: Southern Comfort, water, and peach nectar. I like to add about 3/4 cup (175 ml) pecans for the poaching time.

- Pears poached in 1 ½ cups (375 ml) each water and brandy, with a little fresh ginger OR cardamom to taste.

- Apples poached in 1 ½ cups (375 ml) each apple cider and brandy, with a couple whole cloves, 1 vanilla bean, 2 cinnamon sticks, a pinch of nutmeg, and a handful of dried cranberries.

- ANYTHING poached in mead with zests and juice of satsuma oranges and a little squeeze of fresh lemon juice

Brandied Apple Crisp

Apple crisp was the dish that I was first known for, back when I was a kid. I substituted my favorite granola cereal for the rolled oats that most recipes called for... and a favorite was born! As an adult, I'm a big fan of the combination of apples, cinnamon, brown sugar, and apple brandy - as you may have noticed by now. It just gives a little extra something to this dish. This apple crisp is the perfect way to end a crisp, cool day of apple picking with your special someone!

Sugar	3/4 cup	175 ml
Flour	3/4 cup	175 ml
Granola*	3 cups	750 ml
Butter, melted	1 cup	250 ml
Large, tart apples	7-8	7-8
Apple brandy	1/3 cup	75 ml
Brown sugar, packed	½ cup	125 ml
Cinnamon	½ tsp	125 ml
Walnuts or almonds, optional	½ cup	125 ml

Preheat oven to 375°F (190°C). Grease a 9" square baking dish, set aside.

In a medium bowl, combine sugar, flour, and granola. Add melted butter, stir until well incorporated. Everything should be wet, but crumbly.

Peel (if you want - I don't usually), core, and chop the apples. Toss apple chunks with the apple brandy. Separately, combine brown sugar, cinnamon, and nuts - if using. Add to the bowl of apples, toss until apples are evenly coated.

Spread apple mixture evenly over the bottom of the baking dish. Top with an even layer of the granola mixture, patting down lightly. Bake for 35-45 minutes, or until topping is lightly browned, and apples are tender. Serve with ice cream or whipped cream.

* If you prefer, rolled oats can be substituted for the same amount of granola.

Flavor Ideas:

- While I love this with apple brandy.. try rum, whisky, or whatever else you like. Non-cream liqueurs work best.

-Add sweetened dried cranberries instead of - or in addition to - the nuts.

- For a "Candy Apple" crisp, use sour apple schnapps for the flavoring, add a layer of ½ - 1 cup chopped Kraft caramels on top of the apple layer, before coating with the streusel topping.

- Rather than use apples, try any of the boozy pie fillings, coming up next!

Brandied Apple Crisp

Boozy Pie Fillings

The following recipes are very versatile. Use in place of the apple filling for our boozy apple crisp recipe, or toss in a pastry shell (homemade or store bought) for easy and delicious pies and tarts. Each of these makes one 9" pie worth of filling, or a half batch of Crisp. Double the filling recipe if you'd like to make a full batch of the crisp recipe.

Mixed Berry Filling

Cornstarch	1/4 cup	50 ml
Liqueur of choice*	1/4 cup	50 ml
Sugar	½ cup	125 ml
Fresh strawberries, chopped	1 cup	250 ml
Fresh raspberries	2 cups	500 ml
Fresh blueberries	1 ½ cups	375 ml

In a medium saucepan, combine cornstarch and liqueur, whisking until smooth with no lumps. Add sugar, continuing to whisk until fully incorporated. Heat over medium-low heat until mixture begins to simmer.

Add berries, tossing to coat well with the liquid. Continue to cook for 5 minutes. Remove from heat and allow to cool to room temperature.

To bake into a pie: Line a 9 inch pie plate with a pie crust (store bought, or see recipe on page 188). Fill with berry mixture, top with a second crust, seal the edges.

Cut 2" wide strips of foil, use to cover the edges of the pie crust to prevent burning.

Bake for 25 minutes at 375°F (190°C). Remove foil, return pie to oven, and back for another 20-30 minutes, or until upper pie crust is golden brown. Allow to cool on a wire rack before serving.

* I prefer Chambord or Grand Marnier, but any non-cream liqueur would work well!

Flavor idea: Try adding 2 tsp freshly grated orange or lemon zest for a little zing!

Blueberry Amaretto Filling

Cornstarch	1/4 cup	50 ml
Amaretto	1/4 cup	50 ml
Sugar	3/4 cup	375 ml
Fresh blueberries	4 cups	1000 ml

In a medium saucepan, combine cornstarch and amaretto, whisking until smooth with no lumps. Add sugar, continuing to whisk until fully incorporated. Heat over medium-low heat until mixture begins to simmer. Add blueberries, tossing to coat well with the liquid. Continue to cook for 5 minutes. Remove from heat and allow to cool to room temperature.

To bake into a pie: Line a 9 inch pie plate with a pie crust (store bought, or see recipe below). Fill with berry mixture, top with a second crust, seal the edges.

Cut 2" wide strips of foil, use to cover the edges of the pie crust to prevent burning. Bake for 25 minutes at 375°F (190°C). Remove foil, return pie to oven, and back for another 20-30 minutes, or until upper pie crust is golden brown. Allow to cool on a wire rack before serving.

Southern Comfort Peach Filling

Large ripe peaches	5	5
Cornstarch	1/4 cup	50 ml
Southern Comfort	1/4 cup	50 ml
Fresh lemon juice	2 tsp	10 ml
Sugar	3/4 cup	175 ml

Peel peaches (optional), remove the pit and chop into large chunks.

In a medium saucepan, combine cornstarch, Southern Comfort, and lemon juice, whisking until smooth with no lumps. Add sugar, continuing to whisk until fully incorporated. Heat over medium-low heat until mixture begins to simmer. Add about half of the chopped peaches, tossing to coat well with the liquid. Continue to cook for 5-10 minutes, or until peaches soften and start to break down a bit. Add remaining peaches, continue to cook for 2 minutes. Remove from heat and allow to cool to room temperature.

To bake into a pie: Line a 9 inch pie plate with a pie crust (store bought, or see recipe below). Fill with berry mixture, top with a second crust, seal the edges. Cut 2" wide strips of foil, use to cover the edges of the pie crust to prevent burning.

Bake for 25 minutes at 375°F (190°C). Remove foil, return pie to oven, and back for another 20-30 minutes, or until upper pie crust is golden brown. Allow to cool on a wire rack before serving.

Southern Comfort Peach Pie

Creamy Blueberry Amaretto Pie

This is one of those recipes that I worked out in a dream. Lucid dreaming comes in handy sometimes! I tend to do a lot of problem solving and creative prep work while fast asleep. This isn't a traditional blueberry pie for two reasons:

- The introduction of amaretto adds a new level of complexity to the filling.

- The addition of cream cheese makes the filling almost a cross between a blueberry pie and a cheesecake.

The creaminess works well with the Amaretto and blueberries, and this results in a well-structured pie that doesn't ooze all over the plate. (Once cooled, anyway!) It's delicious warm or cold, and is easy to make.

Cornstarch	1/4 cup	50 ml
Amaretto	1/4 cup	50 ml
Granulated sugar	3/4 cup	175 ml
Fresh blueberries	4 cups	1000 ml
1 brick cream cheese (8 oz), softened		
Amaretto	1/4 cup	50 ml
Large eggs	2	2
Prepared pie crusts	2	2

In a medium saucepan, combine cornstarch and amaretto, whisking until smooth with no lumps. Add sugar, continuing to whisk until fully incorporated. Heat over medium-low heat until mixture begins to simmer. Add blueberries, tossing to coat well with the liquid. Continue to cook for 5 minutes.

Cream together cream cheese, amaretto, and eggs until well incorporated and smooth. Stir into blueberry mixture. Heat, stirring frequently, until mixture comes just to a boil. Remove from heat, allow to cool to room temperature.

Line a 9 inch pie plate with a pie crust (store bought, or see recipe coming up nect). Fill with berry mixture, top with a second crust, seal the edges. Cut a few holes in the top to vent the steam.

Cut 2" wide strips of foil, use to cover the edges of the pie crust to prevent burning.

Bake for 25 minutes at 375°F (190°F). Remove foil, return pie to oven, and back for another 20-30 minutes, or until upper pie crust is golden brown. Allow to cool on a wire rack before serving.

Creamy Blueberry Amaretto Pie

Pie Crust

...and here we are, the final recipe of the book. Interestingly enough, it's not even my own recipe!

Nope, I'm not all that big on making pies, so I asked for my great uncle Tom's permission to publish his special pie crust recipe. He's renowned for his pies, which are reportedly scooped out of his hands on sight!

This recipe is enough to make 3 double crust pies (or 6 single crust pies, obviously!). If you're not intending to make that much pie, no worries - just tightly wrap the dough in foil and freeze it. It'll keep for 3 months in the freezer.

Water	1 cup	250 ml
Large egg	1	1
Vinegar	1 Tbsp	15 ml
Flour	5 ½ cups	1375 ml
Brown sugar	2 Tbsp	30 ml
Baking powder	1 pinch	1 pinch
Salt	1 pinch	1 pinch
Lard*	1 lb	500 g

Whisk water, egg, and vinegar together, set aside. In a larger bowl, mix together flour, brown sugar, baking powder, and salt until well combined.

Add wet ingredients to the bowl of dry ingredients, mixing with a fork until just combined. Add lard, cut in with a pastry cutter or fork gently, until it resembles gravel. Don't over handle it. In Tom's words, "Mix it with kindness"!

Gather dough into a loose ball, divide into 6 equal balls. Wrap each with plastic wrap, and let rest for 30 minutes before using.

Bake, following pie recipe instructions.

* Tom recommends using Tenderflake brand lard, which is apparently only available in Canada. Shortening can be substituted if lard cannot be obtained, but is definitely not preferable to lard.

Conversions

To accommodate bakers in different countries and from different cultures, measurements throughout this book have been provided in both U.S. conventional and metric. To keep things simple, measurement conversions have been rounded. See below for the exact conversions, as well as the rounded versions provided throughout this book.

Spoons	Actual Conversion*	Standard Metric Used
1/4 tsp	1.2 ml	1 ml
½ tsp	2.5 ml	2 ml
1 tsp	4.9 ml	5 ml
1 Tbsp	14.8 ml	15 ml

Cups	Actual Conversion*	Standard Metric Used
1/4 cup	59.1 ml	50 ml
1/3 cup	78.9 ml	75 ml
½ cup	118.3 ml	125 ml
2/3 cup	157.7 ml	150 ml
3/4 cup	177.4 ml	175 ml
1 cup	236.6 ml	250 ml
4 cups	946.4 ml	1000 ml / 1 liter

Ounces (Weight)	Actual Conversion*	Standard Metric Used
1 oz	28.3 grams	30 grams
2 oz	56.7 grams	55 grams
3 oz	85.0 grams	85 grams
4 oz	113.4 grams	125 grams
5 oz	141.7 grams	140 grams
6 oz	170.1 grams	170 grams
7 oz	198.4 grams	200 grams
8 oz	226.8 grams	250 grams
16 oz / 1 lb	453.6 grams	500 grams
32 oz / 2 lbs	907.2 grams	1000 grams / 1 kilogram

* Source: Google Calculator

Resources

This list is for informational purposes only, and does not necessarily constitute an endorsement of any of these companies. We do not receive payment of any kind by these companies for being listed here. It is the readers' responsibility to properly vet any companies they choose to do business with; we are not responsible for any disputes that may arise.

Equipment and Supplies

Country Kitchen Sweet Art
www.countrykitchensa.com
Huge selection of cake decorating supplies. Carries Madeleine pans.

Bar Products dot com
www.barproducts.com
Great variety of bartending supplies.

Ingredients

Futter's Nut Butters
www.futtersnutbutters.com
Various all natural nut butters - Great for truffle making!

Nuts Online
www.nutsonline.com
Nuts, dried fruits, fruit powders, and more.

Other

M. Porter Photography
www.mporterphotography.com
Food, product, and corporate photography
(M. Porter Photography is a division of Celebration Generation LLC)

Index

American Buttercream 71

B-52 Torte 85
Bahama Mama Torte 83
Bananas Foster 176
Bananas Foster Filling for Ravioli 131
Bananas Foster Pralines 156
Bananas Foster Upside-Down Cake 98
Bars
    Nanaimo Bars 150
    Brownies 152
    Rum Raisin Bars 156
Basic Ice Cream 162
Basic Liqueur 17
Basic Dessert Ravioli 127
Basic Sorbet 167
Bellini Cupcakes 80
Berry Filling for Dessert Ravioli 131
Berry Sauce 132
Black Walnut Bread Pudding 96
Blueberry Amaretto Filling 184
Blue Hawaiian Rum Cake 66
Brandied Apples 177
Brandied Apple Crisp 181
Brandied Apple Upside-Down Cake 98
Bread Pudding
    Bread Pudding with Boozy Sauce 89
    Boozy Bread Pudding 90
    Chocolate Bread Pudding 90
    White Chocolate Bread Pudding 92
    White Chocolate Amaretto Sauce...... 92
    Rum Raisin Bread Pudding 93
    Raspberry Peach Bread Pudding 94
    Black Walnut Bread Pudding 96
    Pina Colada Bread Pudding 96
Bread Pudding with Boozy Sauce 89
Brownies 152

Candy
    Bananas Foster Pralines 156
    Margarita Macadamia Brittle 157
    Jalapeno Beer Brittle 158
    Hop Flavored Beer Lollipops 160
Caramel Fondue 52
Caramelized Brandied Pears 175
Chai Infused Vodka 15
Cheesecake Batter 28

Cheesecake Crust 27
Cheesecake Fondue 52
Cheesecakes
    Cheesecake Crust 27
    Basic Cheesecake Batter 28
    Chocolate Chambord 29
    Peachy Southern Comfort 30
    Pina Colada Cheesecake 32
    Grasshopper Cheesecake 33
Cheese Filling for Dessert Ravioli . 130
Cherries Jubilee 178
Chiffon Pies
    Basic Chiffon Pie 46
    Fruit Chiffon Pie 46
    Grasshopper Pie 48
Chocolate Bread Pudding 90
Chocolate Chambord Cheesecake ... 29
Chocolate Chambord Cupcakes 73
Chocolate Creme Brulee 56
Chocolate Cream Pastry Cream 34
Chocolate Dessert Ravioli 128
Chocolate Filling 130
Chocolate Glaze 119
Chocolate Haystack Cookies 148
Chocolate Mousse 43
Chocolate Panna Cotta................. 41
Chocolate Pavlova 173
Chocolate Pudding 38
Chocolate Rum Cake 58
Chocolate Souffle 126
Chocolate Traditional Mousse 46
Citrus Extract 24
Citrus Fondue 50
Cococabana Rum Cake................... 64
Coconut Rum Cake 59
Coffee Infused Vodka 14
Cookies
    Tuiles 122
    Noelles 142
    Fruitcake Cookies 144
    Gluten Free Fruitcake Cookies .. 145
    Chocolate Haystack Cookies 148
Cranberry-Apple Brandy Bundt 70
Creme Brulee
    Basic Creme Brulee 54
    Basic Chocolate Creme Brulee .. 56
Cream Liqueur 20

Cream Liqueur Pastry Cream 34
Cream Puffs 117
Creamy Blueberry Amaretto Pie 186
Cucumber Infused Vodka 15
Cupcakes
    American Buttercream 71
    Swiss Meringue Buttercream 71
    Whisky and Coke Cupcakes 72
    Limoncello Cupcakes 72
    Chocolate Chambord Cupcakes 73
    Lynchburg Lemonade Cupcakes. 74
    Pink Grapefruit Daiquiri Cupcakes .. 76
    Almond Amaretto Cupcakes 77
    Guinness Chocolate Cupcakes 78
    French Martini Cupcakes 78
    Mimosa Cupcakes 79
    Bellini Cupcakes............................. 80

Dark Chocolate Fondue 49
Dark Chocolate Mojito Truffles 115
Dark Chocolate Truffles 107
Dessert Ravioli
    Basic Dessert Ravioli 127
    Chocolate Dessert Ravioli 128
    Fried Dessert Ravioli 130
    Cheese Filling for Dessert Ravioli .. 130
    Chocolate Filling 130
    Bananas Foster Filling 131
    Berry Filling for Dessert Ravioli 131
    Boozy Berry Sauce 132

Eclairs 118
Egg Nog Truffles 114

Fig Infused Brandy 16
Flambe
    Caramelized Brandied Pears 175
    Bananas Foster 176
    Whisky Peaches 176
    Brandied Apples 177
    Mangos Diablo 177
    Cherries Jubilee 178
    Flan 53
Flavor Extracts
    Vanilla Extract 24
    Citrus Extract 24
    Spice Extract 26
    Herbal Extract 26
Fondue
    Dark Chocolate Fondue 49
    Milk Chocolate Fondue 49
    White Chocolate Fondue................ 49
    Tropical Coconut Fondue 50

Citrus Fondue 50
Cheesecake Fondue 52
    Caramel Fondue 52
French Martini Cupcakes 78
Fried Dessert Ravioli 130
Fruitcake, Gluten Free 102
Fruitcake Cookies 144
Fruitcake Cookies, Gluten Free 145
Fruit Chiffon Pie 46
Fruit Flambe 175
Fruit Infused Spirits 12
Fruit Mousse 44
Fruity Panna Cotta 41
Fuzzy Navel Cake 69

Ginger Infused Vodka 16
Gluten Free Fruitcake 102
Gluten Free Fruitcake Cookies 145
Grasshopper Cheesecake 33
Grasshopper Pie 48
Green Tea Infused Vodka 16
Grenadine 20
Guinness Chocolate Cupcakes 78

Herbal Extract 26
Herb Infused Vodka 14
Honey Simple Syrup 19
Hop Flavored Dark Truffles 116
Hop Flavored Beer Lollipops 160

Ice Cream
    Tiramisu Ice Cream 163
    Mint Julep Ice Cream 163
    Mango Mojito Ice Cream 164
    Pina Colada Ice Cream 166
Individual Croquembouche 119
Infused Spirits
    Fruit Infused Spirits 12
    Peanut Infused Rum 14
    Coffee Infused Vodka 14
    Spice Infused Vodka 14
    Herb Infused Vodka 14
    Skittles Infused Vodka 14
    Jalapeno Infused Tequila 15
    Cucumber Infused Vodka 15
    Rose Infused Vodka 15
    Tea Infused Vodka 15
    Chai Infused Vodka 15
    Green Tea Infused Vodka 16
    Vanilla Infused Vodka 16
    Ginger Infused Vodka 16
    Fig Infused Brandy 16

Jalapeno Beer Baklava 123
Jalapeno Beer Brittle 158
Jalapeno Infused Tequila 15

Key Lime Rum Cake 60

Lime Cordial 22
Limoncello Cupcakes 72
Lynchburg Lemonade Cupcakes 74

Madeleines 132
Mango Mojito Ice Cream 164
Mango Mojito Upside-Down Cake 100
Mangos Diablo 177
Maple Simple Syrup 19
Margarita Macadamia Brittle 157
Melon Ball Trifle 138
Milk Chocolate Fondue 49
Milk Chocolate Truffles 108
Mimosa Cupcakes 79
Mini Eclairs 119
Mint Julep Ice Cream 163
Mixed Berry Filling 183
Mousse
   Basic Mousse 43
   Chocolate Mousse 43
   Traditional Mousse 44
   Fruit Mousse 44
   Chocolate Traditional Mousse 46

Nanaimo Bars 150
Noelles 142
Non-Cream Liqueur Pastry Cream 36

Panna Cotta
   Basic Boozy Panna Cotta 40
   Basic Boozy Chocolate Panna Cotta . 41
   Basic Boozy Fruity Panna Cotta 41
Pastry Cream
   Cream Liquor Pastry Cream 34
   Chocolate & Liqueur Pastry Cream . 34
   Non-Cream Liqueur Pastry Cream ... 36
   Chocolate Non-Cream Pastry Cream 36
Pate a choux 117
Pavlova 169
Peachy Southern Comfort Cheesecake 30
Peanut Butter Chip Truffles 111
Peanut Infused Rum 14
Pie Crust 188
Pies
   Mixed Berry Filling 183
   Blueberry Amaretto Filling 184
   Southern Comfort Peach Filling 184

Creamy Blueberry Amaretto Pie 186
   Pie Crust 188
Pina Colada Bread Pudding 96
Pina Colada Cheesecake 32
Pina Colada Ice Cream 166
Pina Colada Rum Cake 62
Pink Grapefruit Daiquiri Cupcakes 76
Poached Fruit 178
Profiteroles 118
Puddings
   Basic Boozy Pudding 38
   Basic Boozy Chocolate Pudding..... . 38

Raspberry Peach Bread Pudding 94
Rose Infused Vodka 15
Rum Cakes
   Basic Rum Cake............................ 57
   Chocolate Rum Cake 58
   Coconut Rum Cake 59
   Key Lime Rum Cake 60
   Strawberry Daiquiri Rum Cake .. 61
   Pina Colada Rum Cake 62
   Cococabana Rum Cake 64
   Zombie Rum Cake 65
   Blue Hawaiian Rum Cake 66
Rum Raisin Bars 156
Rum Raisin Bread Pudding 93
Rum Raisin Truffles 114
Rum Raisin Tarts 154
Rum Runner Trifle 135

Sex on the Beach Torte 81
Simple Syrup 19
Skittles Infused Vodka 14
Souffle 125
Souffle Sauce 127
Southern Belle Torte 87
Southern Comfort Peach Filling ... 184
Southern Peach Upside down Cake 98
Spice Extract 26
Spice Infused Vodka 14
Strawberry Daiquiri Rum Cake 61
Stuffed Strawberries 134
Sugar-Free Truffles 111
Sweet and Sour 22
Swiss Meringue Buttercream 71
Syrups
   Simple Syrup 19
   Honey Simple Syrup 19
   Maple Simple Syrup 19
   Grenadine 20
   Lime Cordial 22
   Sweet and Sour 22

Tea Infused Vodka 15
Tequila Sunrise Cake 68
Tiramisu Ice Cream 163
Tiramisu Torte 86
Tortes
  Sex on the Beach Torte 81
  Bahama Mama Torte 83
  B-52 Torte 85
  Tiramisu Torte 86
  Southern Belle Torte 87
Traditional Croquembouche 120
Traditional Mousse 44
Tropical Coconut Fondue 50
Trifle
  Rum Runner Trifle 135
  Melon Ball Trifle 138
Truffles
  Dark Chocolate Truffles 107
  Milk Chocolate Truffles 108
  White Chocolate Truffles 110
  Peanut Butter Chip Truffles 111
  Sugar-Free Truffles 111
  White Almond Amaretto Truffles ... 112
  Egg Nog Truffles 114
  Rum Raisin Truffles 114
  Dark Chocolate Mojito Truffles 115
  Hop Flavored Dark Truffles 116
Tuiles 122

Upside-Down Cakes
  Basic Upside-Down Cake 97
  Brandied Apple ,,... 98
  Southern Peach 98
  Bananas Foster 98
  Mango Mojito 100
Vanilla Extract 24
Vanilla Infused Vodka 16
Whisky and Coke Cupcakes 72
Whisky Peaches 176
White Almond Amaretto Cupcakes . 77
White Almond Amaretto Truffles .. 112

White Amaretto Bread Pudding 92
White Chocolate Amaretto Sauce ... 92
White Chocolate Fondue 49
White Chocolate Truffles 110
Wine Slush Mix 140

Zombie Rum Cake....................... 65

Marie Porter

Marie Porter is an Autistic polymath, which is just a fancy way of saying that she knows a lot of stuff - and does even more stuff - with a brain that runs on a different operating system than most. Because of that OS, her career has spanned across many facets: She's a trained mixologist, competitive cake artist, professional costumer, and - last but not least - author. As of 2017, her written works include 7 cookbooks, 6 specialty sewing manuals, and a tornado memoir. Her work has graced magazines and blogs around the world, she has costumed for Olympians and professional wrestlers, has baked for brides, celebrities, and even Klingons. Marie is now proud to share her wealth of multi-disciplinary knowledge and experience with cooks and seamstresses around the world

Michael Porter

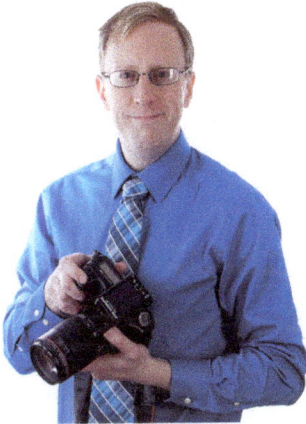

Michael Porter works in medical manufacturing, and is a food and commercial photographer. His work has appeared in local, national, and international magazines, in catalogs, corporate websites, and as well as in many online media outlets. In addition to being an awesome husband and photographer, Michael is Celebration Generation's "Chief Engineering Officer", responsible for all custom builds, equipment repairs, and warp engine emergencies. After their home was smashed by a tornado, Michael singlehandedly built all of the cabinetry in their new kitchen! In his 'spare' time, Michael is an avid home brewer, is pursuing a degree in engineering, and is "in training" to become a Canadian.

Twisted: A Minneapolis Tornado Memoir

On the afternoon of May 22, 2011, North Minneapolis was devastated by a tornado. Twisted recounts the Porters' first 11 months, post tornado. Rebuilding their house, working around the challenges presented by inadequate insurance coverage. Frustration at repeated bouts of incompetence and greed from their city officials. Dealing with issues such as loss of control, logistics, change, and over-stimulation, as autistic adults. With the help of social media – and the incredibly generous support of the geek community – the Porters were able to emerge from the recovery marathon without too much of a hit to their sanity levels. New friends were made, new skills learned, and a "new" house emerged from the destruction. Twisted is a roller coaster of emotion, personal observations, rants, humor, social commentary, set backs and triumphs. Oh, and details on how to cook jambalaya for almost 300 people, in the parking lot of a funeral home… should you ever find yourself in the position to do so!

The Spirited Baker
Intoxicating Desserts & Potent Potables

Combining liqueurs with more traditional baking ingredients can yield spectacular results. Try Mango Mojito Upside Down Cake, Candy Apple Flan, Jalapeno Beer Peanut Brittle, Lynchburg Lemonade Cupcakes, Pina Colada Rum Cake, Strawberry Daiquiri Chiffon Pie, and so much more.

To further add to your creative possibilities, the first chapter teaches how to infuse spirits to make both basic and cream liqueurs, as well as home made flavour extracts! This book contains over 160 easy to make recipes, with variation suggestions to help create hundreds more!

Evil Cake Overlord
Ridiculously Delicious Cakes

Marie Porter has been known for her "ridiculously delicious" moist cakes and tasty, unique flavors since the genesis of her custom cake business. Now, you can have recipes for all of the amazing flavors on her former custom cake menu, as well as many more! Once you have baked your moist work of gastronomic art, fill and frost your cake with any number of tasty possibilities. Milk chocolate cardamom pear, mango mojito.. even our famous Chai cake – the flavor that got us into "Every Day with Rachel Ray" magazine! Feeling creative? Use our easy to follow recipe to make our yummy fondant. Forget everything you've heard about fondant – ours is made from marshmallows and powdered sugar, and is essentially candy – you can even flavor it to bring a whole new level of "yum!" to every cake you make!

Beyond Flour
A Fresh Approach to Gluten-Free Cooking & Baking

Most gluten-free recipes are developed by taking a "normal" recipe, swapping in a simulated "all purpose" gluten-free flour… whether store bought, or a homemade version. "Beyond Flour" takes a different approach: developing the recipe from scratch. Rather than just swapping out the flour for an "all purpose" mix, Marie Porter uses various alternative flours as individual ingredients – skillfully blending flavours, textures, and other properties unique to each flour – not making use of any kind of all-purpose flour mix. Supporting ingredients and different techniques are also utilized to achieve the perfect end goal … not just a "reasonable facsimile". With Beyond Flour, you can now indulge in some of your deepest, darkest guilty pleasure food cravings - safely and joyously!

Hedonistic Hops
The HopHead's Guide to Kitchen Badassery

While hops may seem like a bizarre or exotic item to cook with, they're really not that different from any other herb or spice in your cupboard… you just have to know what to do with them! From condiments, sides, & main dishes, to beverages and desserts, Marie Porter creates delicious recipes utilizing hops of various flavour profiles - playing up their unique characteristics - to create recipes full of complex flavour. Much like salt or lemon juice can be added to dishes to perk them up, a small amount of hops - used wisely, and with specific techniques to do so in a balanced fashion - can really make a dish sing. Even those who are not fans of beer will love the unique flavours that various types of hops can bring to their plate. Floral, earthy, peppery, citrusy…Cooking with hops is a great way to expand your seasoning arsenal!

Beyond Flour 2
A Fresh Approach to Gluten-Free Cooking & Baking

How many times have you come across a gluten-free recipe claiming to be "just as good as the normal version!", only to find that the author must have had some skewed memories on what the "normal" version tasted, looked, and/or felt like?

How many times have you felt the need to settle for food with weird after-taste, gummy consistency, or cardboard-like texture, convinced that this is your new lot in life?

Continuing where its predecessor left off, "Beyond Flour 2" is full of tasty gluten-free recipes that have been developed from scratch to be the absolute best they can be - as good or better than the "real" thing - with no "all purpose" mixes, and no need to compromise on taste or texture!

Sweet Corn Spectacular
(Minnesota Historical Society Press)

The height of summer brings with it the bounty of fresh sweet corn.Grilled or boiled, slathered in butter and sprinkled with salt, corn on the cob is a mainstay of cook-out menus. But this "vegetable" can grace your plate in so many other ways. In fact, author and baker Marie Porter once devised an entire day's worth of corn- based dishes to celebrate her "corn freak"husband's birthday. "Sweet Corn Spectacular" displays Porter's creative and flavor- filled approach to this North American original, inspiring year-round use of this versatile ingredient and tasty experimenting in your own kitchen. As Porter reminds home cooks, the possibilities are endless!

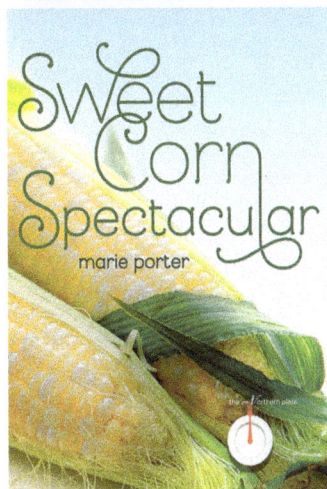

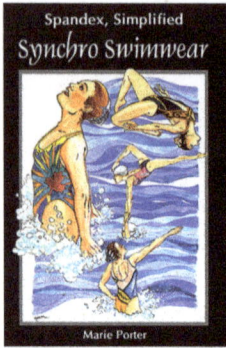

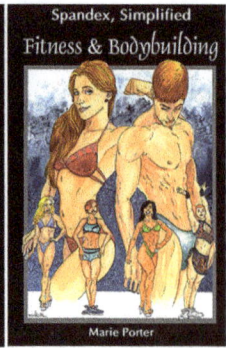

Introducing Marie Porter's "Spandex Simplified" Series

Prior to her cake career, Marie Porter had an illustrious career in spandex costuming. Now, you can learn all of her secrets to spandex design and sewing!

Synchro and recreational swimwear, figure skating attire, gymnastics leotards, fitness / bodybuilding posing suits, superheroes, cosplay , and dancewear are all covered in Marie's new Spandex Simplified series, and are all about designing and creating spectacular and durable competitive sports costuming.

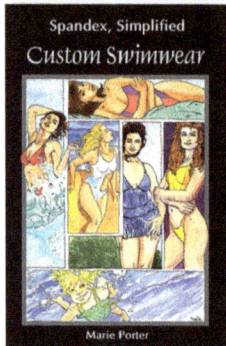

These books are appropriate for beginner to advanced levels of sewing ability,and is written from both a designer, and former "performance" athlete's point of view. They teach everything from the basics, to tricks of the trade. The "Spandex Simplified" series will prepare the reader to design and make almost any design of competitive synchro suit, skating dress, or gymnastics leotard imaginable. Given the cost of decent competition suits, these manuals can pay for themselves with savings from just one project!

The books are written completely in laymans' terms and carefully explained, step by step. Only basic sewing knowledge and talent is required. Learn everything from measuring, to easily creating ornate applique designs, to embellishing the finished suit in one book!

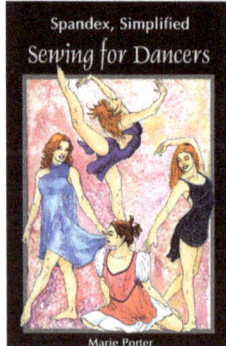

For a complete table of contents listings, current releases, and more info, visit

www.spandexsimplified.com

Wholesale and group purchasing available

www.ingramcontent.com/pod-product-compliance
Lightning Source LLC
Chambersburg PA
CBHW051208090426
42740CB00021B/3425